Flower Therapy

Doreen Virtue
and
Robert Reeves, *N.D.*

HAY HOUSE, INC.
Carlsbad, California • New York City
London • Sydney • Johannesburg
Vancouver • Hong Kong • New Delhi

Published and distributed in the United States by: Hay House, Inc.:
www.hayhouse.com • *Published and distributed in Australia by:* Hay
House Australia Pty. Ltd.: www.hayhouse.com.au • *Published and distributed in the United Kingdom by:* Hay House UK, Ltd.: www.hayhouse
.co.uk • *Published and distributed in the Republic of South Africa by:*
Hay House SA (Pty), Ltd.: www.hayhouse.co.za • *Distributed in Canada
by:* Raincoast: www.raincoast.com • *Published in India by:* Hay House
Publishers India: www.hayhouse.co.in

Cover design: Christy Salinas • *Interior design:* Tricia Breidenthal

The authors of this book do not dispense medical advice or prescribe
the use of any technique as a form of treatment for physical, emotional, or
medical problems without the advice of a physician, either directly or indirectly. The intent of the authors is only to offer information of a general
nature to help you in your quest for emotional and spiritual well-being.
In the event you use any of the information in this book for yourself,
which is your constitutional right, the authors and the publisher assume
no responsibility for your actions.

Library of Congress Cataloging-in-Publication Data

Virtue, Doreen.
  Flower therapy : welcome the angels of nature into your life / Doreen
Virtue and Robert Reeves. -- 1st ed.
       p. cm.
  ISBN 978-1-4019-3968-7 (tradepaper : alk. paper)
  1. Flowers--Psychic aspects. 2. Healing--Miscellanea. I. Reeves, Robert,
N.D. II. Title.
  BF1045.P55V57 2012
  133'.258213--dc23

                          2012004425

ISBN: 978-1-4019-3968-7
Digital ISBN: 978-1-4019-3969-4

15 14 13 12   4 3 2 1
1st edition, August 2012

Printed in China

To nature,
who gave us these
beautiful tools of
love and healing

CONTENTS

INTRODUCTION

What Is Flower Therapy?

Mother Nature is a healer, and one of her most powerful gifts comes in the form of flowers. Each variety has a different "personality" to promote physical and emotional wellness. As Heaven's masterpieces, flowers are Divine vessels of healing, and Flower Therapy is a method of working with different blossoms—based upon their appearance, fragrance, essence, colors, and energies—to address specific needs and desires.

Flower Therapy involves working closely with nature, including the fairies and angels. Fairies make wonderful allies, as they can help you manifest your heart's desires. When you work with flowers, you automatically access fairy energy. Since flowers are home to these elementals, we'll also discuss how to go about picking wildflowers in an energetically responsible way.

I (Doreen) have discussed fairies and angels at length in many of my other books, and in this one, you'll learn about the angels associated with each flower. Angels are

our loving friends, involved in every aspect of our lives, and present throughout the planet. They are filled with joy when they see us utilizing God's healing gifts through working with nature.

Flower Therapy is based upon nature's healing abilities, similar to naturopathic medicine, which is my (Robert's) clinical specialty. Like the herbal treatments in naturopathic medicine, flowers can be used to create potent healing effects.

Since the fragrance and colors of flowers extend into the energetic realm, Flower Therapy helps with metaphysical issues. It can deepen your spiritual practice and open up your psychic abilities. To further this experience, we've included information about giving Flower Therapy readings, which are similar to psychic or angel readings in that they provide guidance and direction for you, your loved ones, and your clients.

Throughout this book, we'll show you methods for working with flower energies, such as sitting next to a particular plant, bathing with specific flower petals, or looking at a photograph of the flower associated with your needs. We'll discuss how to make and use flower essences safely and effectively. Finally, a large portion of this book is devoted to a directory, which lists common flowers and their healing properties.

Everyone can utilize, and benefit from, Flower Therapy. We trust that you'll enjoy this modality and will use this manual as a healing reference tool. Whether you're working with flowers in your own garden, or you purchase them in order to heal a specific situation, they will bring more emotional, physical, and spiritual beauty into your life.

— *Doreen Virtue and Robert Reeves*

PART I

DISCOVERING
FLOWER THERAPY

CHAPTER ONE

FLOWER THERAPY COMPANIONS

Angels and fairies are in every part of nature. The Talmud, an ancient sacred text, says, "Every blade of grass has an angel bending over it, saying 'Grow! Grow!'" Fairies can even be thought of as miniature nature angels. As you enter into the world of Flower Therapy, your spiritual abilities heighten, and you bring yourself into alignment with the angels and fairies. They both serve the environment, so when you work with them for manifestation purposes, your results will skyrocket!

Fairies and Flowers

Working with nature on this deep healing and spiritual level will attune your energy to the fairies. These

beings *do* exist. They're in your garden, your flower bed, and even in the bouquet you purchased from the store. They are very real, and always surround you when you're working with nature.

Think of small, carefree children who are able to enjoy their own company and laugh at anything. This is the vision the fairies hold for you. They ask you to play, and to connect with nature on a deeper level—to go outside, sit in a park, or spend time gardening. Whatever form of nature-based work you do, the fairies are happy to support you. Also, remind yourself to make time every day just to have fun and laugh with your family and friends. Your energy rises with the joy of laughter. It's an excellent feeling!

Folklore often gives fairies a bad name. Please don't listen! Fairies are loving beings of light that want to assist you. They ensure that the planet is being well taken care of. With your heart set on helping the environment, they'll be instantly attracted to you.

Fairies are etheric beings. When compared to other beings of light, though, they are more grounded and connected to Earth energy. This balance allows them to play, and help with Earth-based issues, bringing all of your dreams into physical reality. Ask the fairies to assist you and your family. Anything you request of them can be created very quickly! They're able to speed up your manifestations and bring your desires to fruition.

As you connect with nature and the fairies, you'll start to notice some interesting "unexplained" experiences

4

outdoors. These include seeing small sparkles of light out of the corner of your eye, usually when you're focused intently on your garden or a flower. You'll turn around, but nothing will appear to be there. Please don't attribute this to your imagination. This is a very real fairy sighting! Connecting with nature allows your energetic body to attune to the relaxed feeling of the environment, so you're now in the perfect state to notice the fairies. If you hear voices like children chatting, this means that there are fairies nearby who wish to play with you and make you smile. Seeing flying insects, such as butterflies and ladybugs, is a further indicator that the fairies are working with you.

Fairies are like the guardians of the flowers and the plant kingdom. They watch over every plant, seedling, tree, and shrub, ensuring that they grow and develop as nature has intended. The fairies use healing energies to make the flowers healthy and vigorous.

During meditation you'll see fairies with tiny magic wands, which they use to create flower buds and new shoots. They infuse the flowers with healing and loving energy to help them thrive and blossom; these healing energies will benefit *you* as well. Fairies also help your garden adapt to the seasons. They take care of changing the colors of the leaves and strengthening the plants for the upcoming shifts in weather.

Fairies can watch over your plants and garden while you're away. You need only ask. Like most of us, you have

probably been so busy at times that you have neglected your garden a little. In these cases, you can quickly call upon the fairies and ask them to please look after your plants and flowers. They will happily do so until you're again able to spend more time gardening. When I (Robert) don't have enough time for watering, it will inevitably rain. Miraculously, the sky clouds over and I'm blessed with a shower. This saves me the time and trouble of tending to the garden myself. So call upon the fairies the next time you need to leave your garden, and your helpful friends will keep a watchful eye on your flowers until you return.

Here's a sample (general) prayer:

Prayer to the Fairies

"Dearest Fairies, please guide me as I work with your healing flowers. I wish to choose the perfect ones for me at this time; please help me to do just that. I ask that you surround me with your energy and remind me of the importance of play. I have deep respect and gratitude for all that you do. I pray that I may keep your loving plants happy and healthy with your help."

Angels and Flowers

While fairies are the messengers of Mother Nature, angels are the messengers of God. However, angels are equally connected to the earth; they are part of everything. They're made in the likeness of God, from the same energy as the Divine. God is a part of everything we know, and thus, so too are the angels, who are wonderful, pure energies to work with. Involving them in your daily life brings you many blessings.

The angels are willing to help you with whatever you seek, so include them in your work with flowers. The angels are pure love and light, and aligning with them is very uplifting. When you connect the angels to Flower Therapy, you create a pure healing energy.

As you continue to practice Flower Therapy, you'll discover that each flower has a specific energy. These energies can feel similar to certain archangels, so we have listed the associated archangels for each flower in the Flower Therapy Directory in Part II. Each archangel also has a different aura color. If you feel guided to do so, you may connect archangels to flowers based on their color; however, that is not how they are associated in this book. (For more information on archangels and their aura colors, please see my [Doreen's] book *Archangels 101*.)

Flowers and Chakras

Chakras are energy centers that are located throughout the body—in fact, there are hundreds, if not thousands, of tiny chakras. The seven major chakras, which are larger, are found on the midline of your body up the spine. The energetic vibrations of flowers resonate with the chakras, and you can use these vibrations to help balance and unblock them. Use the charts in Part III to find out which flowers and chakras are related to your situation. More information on chakra clearing can also be found in Chapter 3.

Associating flowers and chakras by physical color would be simple. However, rather than grouping all the purple flowers with the crown chakra and all the indigo flowers with the third-eye chakra, we've instead connected flowers and chakras by their energy and message. If you're unfamiliar with a flower, it could still be useful to match it to a chakra by its color. Please trust your own intuitive guidance, and follow your feelings as to which method will be most healing for you.

CHAPTER TWO

GATHERING AND CARING FOR YOUR HEALING FLOWERS

Flowers are very real, physical displays of love from God and the angels. Upon asking the angels about flowers, we were told, "Flowers are beautiful gifts from the Creator to help you in your times of need. They can help you heal very deep emotional issues and release unhealthy habits. When you trust in your inner voice and Divine guidance, nothing can go wrong." Nature is here to help you, and you have to open your heart to receiving.

We can liken the process of choosing flowers to selecting produce at the grocery store. Trust your gut and go with the choice that *feels* right to you. There's no such

thing as the "perfect flower." Flowers are unique; just like snowflakes, you'll never find two that are identical. Remind yourself that every flower is going to differ slightly from the next. Although you can find apples and oranges that look nearly identical at the supermarket, they were specifically bred to be this way as a means of seeking uniformity. The fruits that didn't fit the standard form were discarded. But if you take a look at organic produce, each piece of fruit is slightly different. Some may have little marks or scratches, and others may not be as vibrantly colored or shiny. Regardless of the external qualities, the energy of the food is going to be the same. (In fact, organic food, with its imperfect, more natural appearance, may have higher nutritional value!) This rings true for flowers as well.

When searching for natural healing tools, you needn't worry about finding a flower with the "perfect" color, shape, or number of petals. Instead, find one that matches the energy of your desire. Flip through the directory in Part II for the types of flowers that best suit your current goals, then go in search of those that you're drawn to.

Sometimes the flowers you find may not look identical to the specimens in this book. Flowers come in all shapes and sizes and can vary dramatically, even from stem to stem of the same plant. You may find a flower that your heart sings for, but when you look at it, perhaps the petals are marked or torn, or it may seem too small. However, you've found yourself mesmerized by this particular

blossom. This is when you must trust your intuition and guidance by choosing this flower because it will be the perfect one for you, the missing piece of the puzzle you've been searching for.

Picking Wildflowers

It can be a lovely and therapeutic experience to pick flowers from the wild. However, before doing so in parks or nature reserves, you must first do a little research to see if it is allowed. These areas are often protected, and picking flowers may be viewed as a type of vandalism. We want to benefit from flowers' healing energies; there's no need to get in trouble for it! Always ask the property owner or the park ranger about the rules for picking flowers. You don't want to accidentally pluck an endangered species!

Remember that you don't need to pick a flower to enjoy the healing energies that are in nature. You can stand or sit nearby for a while to absorb the magical properties that it will share with you. You can also snap photos of flowers that you'll be able to take home with you. Then you can work with these flowers at a later date.

It's important to note that a flower or plant is just as much a living being as you are. It has a very powerful and profound life force that deserves respect and gratitude. If you're able to pick flowers, consider conducting a

flower-picking ceremony. This gives the plant a warning that you're going to cut it, which makes the process of removing the flower more gentle, peaceful, and loving. It also prevents you from disturbing the all-important fairies, and actually *strengthens* your bond with them because they will see how much you care about nature. Fairies are very understanding. If you are having trouble deciding on a flower for your ceremony, make your choice quickly—you will be guided by Divine timing.

When you plan your ceremony, it brings tranquility to your current work. Make this moment calm so that you enjoy the experience. During the ceremony, you're giving love and gratitude to the plant and flower. This helps you elicit even more amazing results when using Flower Therapy, and can enhance healing and manifestation.

The following ceremony is one that we use and recommend:

Flower-Picking Ceremony

You'll need:

- A plant with flowers currently in bloom. This can be one in a pot or in the ground.

- A length of white ribbon about 12 inches (30 centimeters) in length.

- 🏵 A pair of clean, sharp scissors or garden shears. You want to be able to make a quick, smooth cut.

- 🏵 A piece of fruit or cup of juice as a gift to the plant and fairies.

- 🏵 A basket or paper bag so you can carry the flower home.

The evening prior to your ceremony, ask for any additional guidance to come through during your dream time. After waking up, take a shower or bath while holding the intention of cleansing. Clean your physical body along with your energetic one. When you feel cleared and refreshed, you're ready to continue.

Go to the flowering plant before noon; this is when the flower is at its most powerful. Take your harvesting supplies with you and sit or stand in front of the plant. Close your eyes and take several deep breaths.

Say the following prayer:

"Healing plant before me, I come here today to request your assistance. I ask for your healing energies in the form of a flower. I call upon the angels and fairies to please be here with me now. Please assist me during every step of this flower-picking ceremony."

Using your intuition, discern whether this particular plant is right for you to work with today. It's not the right

plant if you feel uneasy or unsure, or if you get a gut feeling of *no*. Honor and respect this guidance. It may mean that another plant of the same species is a better match; perhaps it will even be located nearby. If its energy is more suitable, you will be attracted to it. Trust the answers you receive, and continue making adjustments until you get the right feeling.

Once you've located the right plant, you need to find the right flower. Say the following:

> *"Angels and fairies, please show me, very clearly,*
> *which flower is right for my current situation."*

Again, pay close attention to your intuition. Trust it. Perhaps a butterfly or bee will guide you by landing on a particular flower. Once it flies away, you can continue.

You may be surprised by the flower you're guided to. It may be small or look "imperfect." This is a perception based only on comparisons to the plants you see at the florist. You mustn't get caught up in the physical appearance. The angels say that what's important is the energy of the flower sought.

Measure out enough stem for you to be able to hold the flower comfortably. Tie the white ribbon about 1 inch (2½ centimeters) below where you intend to cut the flower. As you tie the ribbon, say:

> *"Thank you for giving me this beautiful flower*
> *as a gift of healing. With this ribbon I allow*
> *you to prepare for the flower picking."*

Hold your palms over the flower. In your mind's eye, see it glowing white with energy. Envision the fairies and angels adding even more energy to your desires.

When you feel ready to cut the flower, say:

"As I pick this flower, its energy is enhanced and magnified."

Give thanks to the plant by saying:

> *"Thank you for your gift. I will use this*
> *flower with integrity and gratitude."*

Leave some fruit or juice for the plant as a way of saying thank you. This energy helps create new healing flowers.

You can now carry your flower home and work with it using whichever method in the next chapter feels right to you. You have a very pure, sacred gift from nature, the fairies, and the angels. Enjoy the healing and blessings that this gift brings you.

Caring for Your Cut Flowers

Flowers are beautiful and uplifting to be around. They instantly brighten up a room and the mood of everyone in it. You'll want to prolong the length of time you get to enjoy the flowers, as well as how long you're able to benefit from their healing and transformative energies.

However, when you're working with cut or picked flowers, they're eventually going to wilt. How long it takes them to do so depends on *how* you work with them. Sometimes they wilt faster because they are giving all of their energy over to you. This is one of the many gifts that nature gives us. Don't feel bad when your flowers fade; instead, please focus on the gratitude that you hold for nature's help.

Here are a few tricks of the trade that will help extend the life of your flowers:

- Cut the stems underwater, and at a slight angle rather than straight across. You can cut them in a bowl, if that makes it easier.

- Remove any leaves that will sit below the water level in the vase that will hold the flowers.

- Avoid getting water on the petals.

- Add 2 teaspoons of sugar to the water for food, and 1 teaspoon of vinegar to prevent bacteria from growing.

- Every day or two, change the water in the vase.

If you get flowers in florist foam rather than in a vase, you'll need to alter the method slightly. Mix up water and the sugar and vinegar in a jug. Then pour this concoction into the foam.

When flowers are first cut, they can get tiny air bubbles trapped within the stem, which prevents them from absorbing water properly. This results in faster wilting. You can prevent this from happening by always recutting the stems once you get them home (even precut flowers from the store).

Florist Flowers

Flowers from a florist are wonderful to use for Flower Therapy. They're easy to obtain and often very fresh. Freshness means that the cut flowers you're working with will last longer, perhaps longer than those purchased elsewhere, such as a grocery store. Build a relationship with your local florist, who will often be happy to customize bouquets and boxes for you and your family and friends. Imagine how much Flower Therapy florists receive on a daily basis! It would be hard to be anything but cheerful.

Obviously not all of the flowers we mention in this book can be found at a florist. For certain flowers, you'll need to go to your local garden center or nursery or look for them out in nature. A few may be only available regionally. You can also grow your very own flowers at home to experience the joy of seeing them bloom. And remember, it's perfectly okay to use photographs or images of flowers that you can't find.

What to Do with Your Wilted Flowers

Wilting is a natural process in the flower's life—you needn't worry about it. However, please avoid just throwing it in the trash when it reaches this stage. Instead, choose to honor the energy that the flower provided to you by giving back to Mother Earth. Doing so recycles the energy that's being used and allows the earth to make new flowers.

When you're ready, take your wilted flowers to a garden, lawn, or park; leave them on the ground; and say to the earth:

"Thank you for these beautiful gifts of healing and love. I have benefited so much from having these flowers around me. They have given me all that they can, so now it's time to give them back to you. Please take these wilted blossoms and absorb their energy. May you make many more healing flowers. Thank you."

CHAPTER THREE

FLOWER THERAPY HEALING METHODS

Flower Therapy turns healing into a fluid and creative art form that revels in the beauty of flowers' colors, fragrance, and presence. There are as many different Flower Therapy methods as there are varieties of flowers. In this chapter, we offer some tried-and-true techniques.

When you have a particular situation that you wish to address with Flower Therapy, first look through the Flower Therapy Directory in Part II of this book to see which flowers' energy would be appropriate. (If none feel right, see if you are guided to a bloom out in nature or in a photo.) Then use your chosen flower(s) in whichever of

the following methods most appeals to you; your intuition will draw you to the one that will be most energetically effective. Once you're comfortable with these, we encourage you to creatively experiment with other ways to connect with flowers.

Single-Flower Meditation

Choose a single flower. This may be one that you've selected for its healing properties or that you simply feel guided to. Find a comfortable spot to sit where you won't be disturbed and can relax and enjoy your experience. Place the flower on your lap or on a surface in front of you. You can put it in a small vase of water if you like.

Rub your hands together for a few seconds, then hold them over and around the flower. You needn't touch it; just get close enough to connect with its energy. You'll feel a slight change in air pressure or tingling sensations in the palms of your hands as you sense the healing energies. Ask the flower to help you with whatever you need at this time by saying:

"Flower [you may use the flower's name, such as 'Rose'], *please help me with* [describe your concern, such as healing, increasing finances, or attracting romance]. *I'm willing to receive all of the healing, support, and guidance that you have for me. Please allow me to feel the soothing*

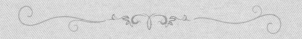

sensations that you bring and to know what messages you have
for me today. I thank you in advance for your wonderful gifts."

Now relax, close your eyes, and breathe deeply. Allow your mind to wander where it needs to go. Notice your thoughts and feelings; they contain healing messages and guidance for you. If you become distracted, gently open your eyes and refocus on the healing flower before you. Sit with it for whatever length of time feels right.

Healing Bath

Hold three flowers in your hands and close your eyes. Think about your desires for healing. When you're ready, gently pluck the petals from the flowers and let them fall into a bathtub filled with warm water. Soak in the bath for at least 15 minutes. (If you're uncomfortable placing the flowers directly into the water, arrange them around the edge of the tub or on the floor. The energy will fill the room, and your body will still absorb it.)

When you're finished, pat yourself dry and collect the petals. Sprinkle them on the ground outside, thanking the flowers as you do so.

Flower-Fragrance Focusing

Sit with a single flower and close your eyes. Inhale its delicate perfume and energy. When you're done, hold the blossom close to your chest (perhaps by placing it in your bra or shirt pocket) so that you can continue breathing its healing fragrance throughout the day.

House Clearing

Gather some of the flowers with clearing properties as listed in Part II and in the Flower Therapy Charts in Part III. For example, you can use orange lilies for releasing heavy energy and white roses for cleansing and purification. Position the flowers in a main area of the house, such as a living room or dining room. Place the flowers in a nice vase in a clearly visible location. Next, hold your hands over the flowers and say:

"Please allow these flowers to clear any and all negative energies, any and all blockages, and bring balance back into this home. Allow this clearing to be fast, effective, and gentle to my family and me. Thank you."

Leave the flowers in the room until they wilt. Remember to change their water frequently. They may wilt faster as they absorb the negativity from your home. After this happens, be sure to thank them as you remove them from the vase.

Chakra Balancing

Gather seven flowers, in each color of the rainbow (red, orange, yellow, green/pink, light blue, dark blue, and purple), to represent the chakras. Alternatively, you can choose seven flowers that represent the properties of each chakra as shown in the following chart. You can even choose seven of the same flowers and hold the intention that each one heal and support a different chakra.

CHAKRA	LOCATION	CORRESPOND-ING ISSUES	COLOR	EXAMPLE OF CORRE-SPONDING FLOWER
Crown	Inside the top of the head	Claircognizance and Divine guidance	Royal purple	Tulip
Third eye	Between the eyes	Clairvoyance	Dark blue	Jasmine
Throat	Adam's apple	Communication, speaking your truth	Light blue	Daffodil
Heart	Chest	Love, clairsentience	Emerald green	Red rose
Solar plexus	Stomach area	Power and control	Yellow	Gerbera
Sacral	3 to 4 inches below the solar plexus	Physical desires and appetites, addictions	Orange	Camellia

CHAKRA	LOCATION	CORRESPOND-ING ISSUES	COLOR	EXAMPLE OF CORRE-SPONDING FLOWER
Root	Base of spine	Survival and sustenance concerns, such as money, shelter, and basic material needs	Red	Daisy

Lie on a bed comfortably, relax, and be open to receiving the Flower Therapy chakra balancing. Next, place the flower corresponding to each chakra upon that location of your body. You can have someone else place the flowers on you if you prefer. Hold the intention that the flower help with issues related to that chakra. Begin with your root chakra. Wait at least two minutes before placing the next flower on your sacral chakra. Breathe deeply. Continue with the remaining flowers, giving each one two minutes or more to be absorbed into the chakra before moving on to the next.

After 15 minutes or more, slowly remove each of the flowers. Start at the root chakra and work up to the crown. Take your time sitting up. Thank the flowers for the balance, and then scatter them outside on the grass or in a park. Chakra balancing is healing and detoxifying, so be sure to drink plenty of water afterward.

Aura Stroking

Choose a flower that's clearing and purifying, such as a white rose. Slowly move the flower around your entire body, through your aura. Doing so will clear out any lower energies from your aura, along with any stress or tension. In this way, your Divine light will shine more brightly, allowing you to be of greater service.

Pillow Flower Therapy

Sprinkle your pillows with the liquid essence of the flower associated with the healing properties you desire (see the next chapter for information on creating these essences). You can also place petals inside your pillowcase. As you're falling asleep, ask the flower to bring its healing properties into your dreams. Lavender is particularly effective when placed on your pillow, as it inspires deep, restorative sleep.

Flower Photos

Depending on where you live, some flowers are easier to obtain than others. However, the angels say that you don't need physical flowers in order to work with flower energy. You can find a photo of the flower and use it as

you would a physical bloom. Sit with the photo, gaze at it, admire it, and allow the flower's energy to inspire you.

To enhance your own healing benefits, carry photos of the flowers specific to your needs. Place these at your work space, near your bed, or on the refrigerator. Trust your guidance, and include flower images wherever you feel they are needed. The pages in this book are filled with the loving energy and healing messages that flowers have to offer. By simply gazing at the photos in Part II, you'll feel Flower Therapy beginning to work. You can also randomly turn to a page from the directory as a divination oracle when you need guidance.

Flower Therapy Seeds

Head to your local garden center and purchase some good-quality flower seeds. Before you plant them, infuse the seeds with your positive and heartfelt intentions. You're communicating with nature and asking for assistance in any areas where it's needed. Hold the seeds in the palm of your hand. In your mind's eye, create an image of yourself being totally happy and healthy. Imagine your wishes being granted. Hold this image for as long as you can. You can ask the seeds to help with a specific request, such as healing, increasing clairvoyance, or attracting abundance. You don't need special words; your intentions and emotions are enough. The seeds can hear those thoughts and are listening to your request. When you feel

ready, plant the seeds in a garden bed or pot. Water them every few days and enjoy watching them sprout and grow. The larger they become, the more energy they feed into your desires and wishes.

Flower Therapy Garden

Dedicate a special area of your garden to Flower Therapy plants. You can choose to cultivate a variety of flowers that will help with your current situation, or plant just one kind of flower and experience its energy being multiplied. Allow nature to guide your healing plants. The fairies and nature spirits will bring health and vitality to everything in your garden and help care for it. Enjoy making this area a beautiful healing space with gorgeous blossoms, statues, and crystals.

If you don't have a garden space, you can still enjoy this form of Flower Therapy. Fill a few pots or planters with the flowers of your choosing and place them around your home, perhaps on your windowsill or a balcony. You may choose to have one or several different flowers growing together.

Your Flower Therapy garden will be a peaceful and fun place to meditate and connect with your angels. Sitting by your healing flowers will dissolve any stress or concern. Aim to spend as much time with them as possible.

Sending Flowers to Others

Do you have a friend or family member whom you'd love to help? Is there someone to whom you'd really like to give some healing, loving energy? As a sensitive person, you may find it challenging to watch friends and loved ones who are struggling and in need. They can be too proud or stubborn to let you help them. To respect their wishes, you need to take a step back and wait for them to ask you for your help.

In these types of situations, Flower Therapy can be wonderfully healing and transformative. Simply send a bouquet to your loved ones; then they'll be able to benefit from the energy that your chosen flowers have to offer. It's truly a wonderful gift that you can give to someone, and people rarely refuse flowers.

When using Flower Therapy as a healing tool, you can perfectly tailor the flower arrangement to suit the situation. For example, send a bunch of gladioli to heal grief, sunflowers to lift depression, or yellow lilies for financial support. Ask your local florist to customize the flowers to your needs. You don't need to tell your loved ones why you've sent them flowers or what the flowers do. Rest assured that the healing process is in motion. Now you can sit back and enjoy the miracles that will follow.

CHAPTER FOUR

FLOWER ESSENCES AND INFUSIONS

Flower essences are energetic medicines that work on a vibrational level. They help to first anchor changes in your energetic field, then bring them to the physical level. When prepared correctly, essences don't contain any physical properties of the flowers. Instead, as in homeopathy, you are transfusing the flower's energy, sending only its energetic blueprint into water. Rest assured that what you're ingesting is very safe and won't interfere with any other medications that you're currently taking.

Before making flower essences, be sure that you are well rested and have all your supplies ready. Gather fresh flowers of your choosing. It's best to use one type per essence. Picking flowers from their native habitat is ideal,

but it's fine to buy those you can't find. It is your heartfelt desires and intentions that make this process work, so it doesn't matter where the flowers come from. Gather the flowers right before you make the essence so that they're fresh.

You will also need:

- ❀ A glass bowl
- ❀ A glass cup that will fit inside the bowl
- ❀ Amber-glass dropper bottles (0.5 fl. oz./15 mL capacity)
- ❀ Pure springwater
- ❀ Brandy or glycerin as a preservative

It is best to do this work on a sunny morning. Head toward a nice, somewhat secluded area where you won't be disturbed. Parks are often good places for this purpose. Be sure that you have a clear view of the sun and that your essence won't get knocked over by passersby.

Once at your location, place the glass bowl on the ground. Make sure it's stable and there isn't any debris below it that might cause a fire. (The power of the sun can be magnified when refracted through glass and water.) Arrange your other supplies nearby.

Sit, then hold your flowers above the bowl and close your eyes. Ask for the flowers to become an essence by saying:

> *"Flowers, please send your healing energies and
> powerful vibrations into the water. I call upon the angels
> and the fairies to assist in this process. I ask you to
> ensure that only healing love and light be sent into
> the water. Everything else is dissolved."*

Now place as many flowers as you can into the cup without squashing them, and place the cup inside the bowl. Carefully pour the springwater into the bowl. The level of the water should be higher than some of the flowers in the cup, but none should actually flow into it. You should have a cup of flowers sitting in a bowl of water, with no flowers touching the water. This "indirect" method of creating essences makes it very easy and safe to use. The energy of the flowers easily passes through the glass.

Allow the flowers to sit in the sunlight for at least four hours. Afterward, offer them gratitude for their service by saying:

> *"Thank you, flowers, for allowing me to spread
> your love and light in new and exciting ways."*

Now carefully remove the cup from inside the bowl. You can spread the flowers on the grass around you to return them to Mother Earth. The liquid that remains in the bowl is no longer ordinary water: it's a powerful essence of the flowers' energy and vibration. It is called the Mother Essence. To stabilize the energy of the Mother Essence, fill the amber-glass dropper bottles half with your

Mother Essence and half with your preservative (brandy or glycerin). Cap the bottles, and give them a good shake to mix the liquids.

Try tasting some of this raw liquid. Notice the feeling and vibrations that come over you.

Making a Stock Bottle

To use your essence, you'll first need to make a stock bottle. Doing so enhances the energy of the essence, making it stronger and more effective.

Fill the amber-glass dropper bottles with preservative (brandy or glycerin). Add five drops of the Mother Essence to each stock bottle. Cap the bottles, and shake well.

Let the stock bottles rest for a few minutes before using. This ensures that the energy is spread through the liquid. You can also surround your stock bottles with clear quartz crystals to enhance the energy of the essence.

You can use your finished stock bottles in a number of ways:

❀ Create a personal dosage bottle: Fill an amber-glass bottle with ⅓ preservative (brandy or glycerin) and ⅔ springwater; add 5 drops stock essence. (You can add up to eight different stock essences to a single dosage bottle.) The recommended dosage is 5 drops under the tongue two to three times

per day, but you can take a dose as often as you feel guided to.

- ❀ Add 5 drops to your drinking water, and sip it over an hour or two.
- ❀ Place a few drops in your palms. Rub your hands together and feel the energy.
- ❀ Add 5 drops to a watering can and then water your garden.
- ❀ Add 5 drops to a spray bottle. Mist this through your own aura and your home.

Infusions

Infusions are herbal teas that are made with love and a firmly held intention. Drinking the infusion brings the energy of the flower into your body and is a wonderfully relaxing way to benefit from Flower Therapy. The process of making the tea can start the relaxation response. Not all of the flowers in the directory are suitable for consumption. However, the following healing herbs and flowers can be used for infusions:

- ❀ Calendula
- ❀ Chamomile
- ❀ Dandelion Leaf
- ❀ Dandelion Root

- ❀ Echinacea Root
- ❀ Eucalyptus Leaf
- ❀ Hibiscus Flower
- ❀ Jasmine
- ❀ Lavender
- ❀ Passionflower
- ❀ Rosebuds
- ❀ Rose Hips
- ❀ Saint-John's-Wort

Please only use herbs purchased from a reputable source. Choose those that are labeled as specifically for tea drinking. There are many different species of plants, and some similar-looking ones can be very different in their chemical structures, so be cautious regarding wild herbs and flowers.

You can enjoy the infusion as a single-ingredient tea, or brew your own magical potion by mixing a little of several herbs. The general guideline is to use 1 teaspoon of dried herbs for each cup of water. To make your own Flower Therapy infusions, follow the recipe on the next page.

Making an Herbal Infusion

1. Boil some springwater or purified water.

2. Measure out 1 teaspoon of your chosen herb(s) for every cup of water you use. Add the herbs to a teapot or metal infuser ball. You can add the herbs directly to the cup instead; this will simply require you to strain the tea before drinking.

3. Add a small amount of cold water to the teapot or cup to prevent scorching the plant. Then add the boiling water.

4. Put the lid on the teapot, or place a saucer over the top of your cup. This prevents steam from escaping and makes a better infusion.

5. Allow to infuse for 15 minutes. Remove the saucer or plate, and strain if necessary. Enjoy your Flower Therapy infusion!

Some Flower Therapy Infusion Blends

To enhance psychic ability

- ❀ Lavender
- ❀ Echinacea Root
- ❀ Jasmine

For romance

* Rosebuds

For calming

* Lavender

* Chamomile

* Saint-John's-Wort

For family unity

* Hibiscus Flower

* Dandelion Leaf

For energy clearing

* Echinacea Root

* Calendula

* Jasmine

CHAPTER FIVE

FLOWERS AND DIVINE GUIDANCE

Divination is the art of gaining answers from the Divine. It's a practice that has been around for centuries, and flowers are one of the oldest tools used. Today, we see oracle cards at the forefront of the divination world. They're wonderfully simple and effective; with just a shuffle, you can quickly get an answer to your question. Oracle cards also tend to have detailed messages associated with them, making them easy to interpret. Another divination practice is to drip wax into water, then watch what forms the cooled wax takes. Yet another ancient method is the use of runes, which are hand-carved from small stones, each with a particular meaning or message. The runes are chosen at random or tossed in front of you to indicate your answer.

Divination works through the Law of Attraction. Each time you gather information from the Divine, the perfect messages come through. Whenever you ask for an answer to your question, the Universe will give you very clear guidance. Because the process is Divinely guided, you can never make a mistake. The Law of Attraction always brings the right information directly to you.

Flower Divination

As we said, flowers have long been used by many people as a divination tool—even by people who had no idea they were connecting to the Creator. Think of a child chanting "He loves me, he loves me not" while picking flower petals. In the same way, Flower Therapy divination works best when a yes-or-no question is posed.

The process is simple:

1. Ask the angels a question, and phrase it in a yes-or-no format. This can be anything that's on your mind. You don't need any special words or prayers to connect to the angels; all you need is an open heart and mind.

2. Choose a flower that you feel drawn to.

3. Gently pluck the petals from the flower. Alternate between saying "yes" and "no" each time you remove a petal.

4. When you pluck the final flower petal, the word you end with is your answer.

This simple method can be made even more powerful by choosing a flower with the vibrational properties connected to your question. For example, if your question surrounds love, gather the energy of a red rose. You can pick the flower from the place it grows or purchase it from a florist. It doesn't matter which method you choose; the energy is the same either way. The healing messages are still there within each flower.

If you're not sure what to ask, you might pick from the following questions:

- ❀ *Is this practitioner right for me?*

- ❀ *Is this course or workshop going to help me improve my spirituality?*

- ❀ *Should I gather more information about this situation?*

- ❀ *Am I on the right path?*

- ❀ *Does my romantic partner have my best interests at heart?*

- ❀ *Should I take this job?*

Flower Therapy Readings

Flower Therapy readings are very simple to perform and wonderfully beneficial—not only for yourself, but also for your family, friends, and colleagues. Everyone can benefit from the healing energy that flowers have to offer.

Right now, you might be hearing your ego's voice telling you that you're incapable of doing Flower Therapy readings. Don't listen to it. Just take a few deep, cleansing breaths and allow yourself to relax. Bring yourself to a state of greater relaxation and peace. It's in this state that you're able to more clearly hear the voices of your angels. They're shouting that you certainly *can* give and receive Flower Therapy readings!

Many people feel that in order to give accurate readings, they need to have had clairvoyant abilities all their lives. But we want to let you in on a little secret: *everyone* is psychic! You were born with the gift of intuition, and you have the same insight that every well-known psychic has. They don't have anything special up their sleeves; you're just as good as they are. The big difference is that they *know* they're psychic and trust the information that they're given. You may be a little doubtful of your guidance in the beginning, but continue to practice anyway. Say everything that you hear, see, feel, or think. You'll quickly come to realize that yes, you too are quite psychic.

Nature, God, and the angels are ready and willing to help. When they sense your true intentions, they

instantly help you to the best of their abilities—which is mighty powerful indeed! Set your focus on helping and healing others, then their messages will come through in a very pure and accurate way. Remember that readings are done to offer guidance and healing, not as a way to impress your friends or family members. In a reading, you are looking for the cause of others' current concerns and seeking guidance as to how they can move through a difficult time. Heal their concerns in the quickest and most efficient way, and connect your clients to love.

When you begin conducting Flower Therapy readings, you may want to adhere to the methods described below. This is just a guideline for you to get started, so if you feel there's a need to change something or jump ahead, then please do. Continue until you feel confident and comfortable with the process, then use your creative flair and make it your own.

Before any reading, please make sure you're clear and focused. You can achieve this through a number of ways, such as by clearing and balancing your chakras. As discussed in Chapter 3, this is a great habit to fall into, because it has you ready for doing readings all the time. Although there are numerous tiny chakras all over your body, you need only clear the seven major chakras. This causes a ripple effect that clears through all the lesser chakras. It also helps bring more balance to your life in terms of work, rest, and play. There are many methods

that you can use to clear your chakras. We've just listed a few choices for you here:

Chakra-Clearing Methods

❀ Use sprays made from flower essences.

❀ Enjoy sea-salt baths.

❀ Swim in the ocean.

❀ Lie on the grass for ten minutes.

❀ Drink flower essences or infusions.

❀ Pass a white rose over your chakras and aura.

❀ Point a clear quartz crystal at each chakra for a moment.

❀ Call upon the angels.

Here is a fast, simple method of clearing your chakras through invoking the purifying energy of Archangel Michael:

Archangel Michael Chakra-Clearing Prayer

Take a few deep breaths and close your eyes. It's best if you're able to sit in a quiet space where you won't be disturbed for a few minutes.

Ask Archangel Michael to clear the energy of your chakras. As he does, continue to breathe deeply. Bring your attention to your root chakra, then say:

*"Archangel Michael, please cleanse
and balance my root chakra."*

Take a deep breath in, hold it for a second, then release the breath. As you exhale, let go of any negativity that may have been lodged within you. Continue using this method and prayer as you move through the sacral, solar-plexus, heart, throat, third-eye, and crown chakra.

Finally, take another deep breath, hold it for a moment, then release it. Say:

*"Thank you, Archangel Michael, for releasing
this heaviness from my body and aura. Thank
you for bringing balance to my chakras."*

Performing a Flower Therapy Reading

When doing a reading for someone else, it's important to prepare beforehand. You never want to bring a rushed energy into your reading space. Quietly sit with the person you're doing a reading for, and convey loving and compassionate energy to him or her. Never make the other person feel hurried.

A common misconception is that you are supposed to know everything. However, a psychic never knows every detail of a situation; rather, you merely serve to pass on messages from Heaven. If you're feeling confused, feel free to ask questions or solicit more details from the person

receiving the reading. These will only help you give even more accurate and detailed answers.

To begin a reading, find a comfortable space where you won't be disturbed. If you're doing this for a friend or client, provide him or her with a comfortable seat. Take a pen and paper with you to jot down notes.

Take a few deep breaths until you feel relaxed and ready. Then call upon the angels by saying:

"Angels, please be here with me now. Support me during this Flower Therapy reading. I call upon Archangel Michael to help cast out all fear energy. Please give me confidence so that I may deliver these healing messages. Please allow all of the information to come through clearly and accurately, and ensure that my client will be able to understand your guidance. I ask that this reading be filled with love and healing in all ways. And so it is."

Silently ask a question in your mind, sending it to the angels and Mother Nature. This may be a specific question such as, "What is preventing [client's name] from getting a new job?" You can also ask something more general, such as, "What does _____ need to know right now?"

Relax and wait for information to come through. It may come as thoughts, visions, words, or feelings. You may write down the messages as they come through, or say them out loud.

Visualize the angels standing in front of you, holding beautiful bouquets of flowers. Look closer and take note of which flowers are in the bouquets. You may want to write these down. You'll usually receive impressions as to what each flower does, but you may also want to look in the directory in Part II for more information.

Alternatively, after asking your question, you can open this book at random. Intuitively turn to one of the flowers and read the healing message that it has for you. This will guide you to your answers.

Afterward, remember to give a healing prescription to derive even greater benefits from the reading. The flowers that you visualized or turned to in this book are the ones that you or your client should continue working with. For example, if you're seeking new love and romance, the reading will probably guide you to the energy of red roses. So, after the reading, you would begin working more closely with the energy of roses. You could display bouquets of them in your home, and carry photos in your pocket or wallet. Use them in any of the Flower Therapy methods that you are attracted to.

Flower Therapy readings are a lovely gift for yourself . . . or anyone at all. They're so uplifting and enjoyable for both you and the recipient.

PART II

FLOWER THERAPY DIRECTORY

FLOWERS THAT AREN'T MENTIONED IN THIS BOOK

Every flower has the potential to be a healing tool for Flower Therapy. Obviously we only have so much room in this book, so we've chosen 88 of our favorites. Most people will be able to obtain the majority of these flowers easily. For any that you can't find, you can either use a photo of the desired flower or substitute baby's breath or dianthus.

Don't think that the flowers that go unmentioned aren't as good or powerful to work with. We encourage you to explore your continued bond with Mother Nature on a deeper level. Discover how local flowers can provide you with profound healing experiences.

You may not know the name of a particular flower, yet for some reason you keep being drawn to it. Trust this inner guidance, and allow yourself to work with the flower. You may find it very therapeutic. Do a little research before you begin using it: It may be advisable not to touch the bloom directly and instead only look at it. For example, you might like the look of one growing in poison ivy; however, it's best to leave it where it is! Don't gather any flowers at the risk of harming yourself.

You can use the following method to discover the healing energy of a particular flower that is not mentioned in this book:

1. Find a representation of the flower you want to know more about. Ideally this will be a physical, fresh flower. If you can't locate one, then try using a photo or image of the flower.

2. Sit with the flower, even if it's just in a photo or if it's still attached to the plant outside.

3. Close your eyes and take several deep breaths with the intention of connecting to the flower.

4. When you're ready, open your eyes and gently gaze at the blossom. Enjoy sitting with it. Notice any thoughts or impressions

that come to mind, as well as how you're feeling at this moment.

5. If you want more information, simply ask the flower to tell you what it can help with. Sit and relax, allowing the information to come to you naturally.

6. Once you feel complete, thank the flower for the information you've received. Now you can work with this flower on a deeper level and also better understand why you felt drawn to it. Interestingly, a flower that you use this method on will often possess the qualities relating to what you're currently going through—it will serve as a perfect friend given to you by nature.

THE DIRECTORY

In this directory are detailed descriptions of 88 healing flowers that can be used for Flower Therapy. Here is the outline of what to expect in each entry.

Image

Each entry includes a photograph of the flower being discussed. You can use this as one of your healing tools by sitting and gazing at it. You'll feel the healing energies coming through the pages of the book and into your body. Each image has been infused with the signature energy of the flower in question.

Description

Under the main heading, which identifies the most common name that a flower is known by, you will find the following information:

Alternative Names: If there is more than one common name that a flower is known by, we include them here.

Botanical Name: This is the genus and species name of the flower. If "spp." is listed after the genus, this means that several species of a flower are being referred to rather than a particular one.

Common Varieties: When many species of the same flower family are referred to, we will sometimes list the most common ones that you will encounter.

Energetic Properties: These are the energetic and healing properties of each flower.

Associated Archangels: Listed here are the archangels connected to the energy of this flower.

Associated Chakras: These are the chakras connected to the energy of this flower.

Healing Description: This lists what kind of healing this flower can be used for. Sometimes you'll find healing tips in this section specific to each flower.

Message from the Flower: This is a channeled message directly from the flower. Read this as though the flower is speaking directly to you. It may hold the answer to your questions.

African Violet

Botanical Name: *Saintpaulia* spp.

Energetic Properties: Cleansing, purification, clearing homes and offices, and transmuting energy from low to high

Associated Archangels: Chamuel, Metatron, Michael, and Raphael

Associated Chakras: Third eye and crown

Healing Description: African Violets are wonderful for healers and psychics because they are excellent cleansers of old, heavy energies. They're great at cleaning spaces, such as homes and offices, as well as your own physical body. Place them on your bedside table to gently remove negativity while you sleep. You can also clear away old energy by placing one or more Violets in a room and saying, *"Healing flower, please transform all lower energies within this space/body. Return them to their rightful state of love and light. Thank you for this healing."*

To keep them happy and healthy, the Violets request that you please allow them to bask in gentle sun at least once a week.

Message from African Violet: "I'll cleanse away the old and give life to the new. This is a long-overdue process. Allow me to help you with this healing process and remove old, stagnant, negative energies. I can transmute the lower forms of energy within your body and home and return them to their positive state of peace and love. You'll notice this subtle yet powerful change. You're sure to enjoy and appreciate this cleansing upon completion."

Agapanthus

Botanical Name: *Agapanthus* spp.

Common Varieties: Lily of the Nile (*Agapanthus africanus*) and African lily (*Agapanthus praecox*)

Energetic Properties: Environmental healing, balancing the energy of the earth, healing global issues, encasing the entire situation with love, releasing addictions, clearing habits, removing old belief patterns, and granting wishes

Associated Archangels: Ariel and Raphael

Associated Chakra: Root

Healing Description: Agapanthus flowers look like a large ball. They come in either purple or white; both colors bring the same healing energy. The vibration of the Agapanthus is that of global healing, which is hinted at in the globe-like shape of the flower head. This flower is excellent at healing and regulating the energy of the earth, especially as we go through transition phases. It helps heal situations in their entirety; just think of the whole, or "global," extent of the affair.

You can work with this flower to clear the energy of deeply ingrained issues. For example, it can help release old belief patterns or clear the energy of addictions. These kinds of issues can be spread through many areas of your life, so it's important to make sure you clear out every last remnant. You can use the long-stemmed flowers as giant wands for granting wishes—just imagine yourself as the good witch from *The Wizard of Oz*.

Message from Agapanthus: "I can be of immense assistance to any global healing that is needed. After any kind of significant world event, I can be here with you. I serve to help regulate and bring balance to the energy. It's normal and natural for the world's energy to shift from time to time, but I can make this transition much easier and more comfortable for you. I would love to play a role in this transition for you. I'll be there as your support during these events, releasing the old and bringing you closer to God.

"I encase the entire situation in love. I bring peace and harmony right now, along with loving energy, to each and every person who is involved. If you have some kind of issue you'd like to see resolved, I'll help. I can be of service by providing you with healing energies to mend it in its entirety."

Anthurium

Alternative Name: Flamingo flower

Botanical Name: *Anthurium* spp.

Common Varieties: Flamingo lily (*Anthurium andraeanum*) and obake anthurium

Energetic Properties: Enhancing passion, love, and romance; increasing sensuality; spreading the word of love; and helping you choose loving words

Associated Archangels: Gabriel and Jophiel

Associated Chakras: Heart and throat

Healing Description: The Anthurium is a heart-centered flower that focuses its energy on love and passion, which helps you connect on a deep level. Anthurium then spreads that energy to those around you. Listen to the adage "Lead by example." You're able to display the peaceful nature that love can bring, and thus inspire others to choose this same path for themselves.

Anthurium flowers last awhile after being cut from the plant. Perhaps this is due to the importance of Anthurium's healing message. Maybe God feels as though this flower needs to remain with you longer so you can truly appreciate what it is capable of.

Message from Anthurium: "I enhance passion, sensuality, and romance. I allow you to open up your heart and connect deeply to other human beings, conveying the true message of love to them. I guide you through your caring actions, words, and choices. Now is the time for you to connect to this deep sense of love. You may then assist others who are joining you in this state of bliss, which is a very natural process that I merely wish to facilitate.

"Share with the world the rivers of love that flow within you. You're now connecting to your Divine passion, through which you're able to inspire others. I'll help you choose your words so that they give forth the most loving energy they can. This will spread among your fellow men and women so that they, too, begin to choose their words with love."

Azalea

Botanical Name: *Rhododendron* spp.

Energetic Properties: Wisdom, spiritual understanding, clearing past-life issues, and deep meditation

Associated Archangel: Raziel

Associated Chakra: Crown

Healing Description: This flower is connected to deep spirituality and wisdom. Its energy is gentle and subtle, yet profound nonetheless! When working with the energy of Azalea, you'll be taken on a journey that's individual to you. It will help you learn more about yourself and your personal history, including your past lives.

Planting a garden of Azaleas can assist you in deepening your spirituality. You may even choose to obtain an Azalea bonsai, which is very magical and makes a wonderful meditation tool.

Message from Azalea: "I'll gently take your hand and guide you along the path of spirituality. With me by your side, you can release any blockages to your God-given spiritual abilities. Open up to a world of wisdom. I respect the process of this journey, so I'll never rush you. I'll help you focus on absorbing each lesson, one at a time, so you're constantly learning, yet never feeling pushed out of your comfort zone. You've been spiritual and connected to nature throughout many lifetimes, and I would like to remind you of this. When I'm around, I can assist you in clearing up any unresolved past-life issues. Together, we can continue learning through the path of spirituality."

Baby's Breath

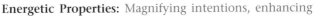

Alternative Name: Chalk plant

Botanical Name: *Gypsophila* spp.

Energetic Properties: Magnifying intentions, enhancing the energy of other flowers, and anchoring energy

Associated Archangels: Metatron, Michael, and Uriel

Associated Chakras: All

Healing Description: Baby's Breath is so helpful when using Flower Therapy. If another flower is expensive or difficult to find, you can substitute Baby's Breath. It's almost as though the tiny white blossoms transform into the flower you wish to work with. If you choose to use photographs, place some Baby's Breath on top to augment the energy of the underlying flower. Baby's Breath also magnifies the energy of objects such as crystals.

The ability of Baby's Breath to help anchor the energy of a situation is why you'll often see it in wedding bunches and displays. It activates the romance energy of the room and strengthens the commitment that's being made.

Message from Baby's Breath: "I am a catalyst of the energy of flowers, objects, and situations. Please make use of me; I want to help. If you can find only small amounts of something you desire, I'll magnify the energy a hundredfold. I will ground the situation and affirm that everything is as it should be."

Banksia

Botanical Name: *Banksia* spp.

Energetic Properties: Starting anew; releasing the past; moving on from difficult times, including divorce, heartache, job changes, and health challenges

Associated Archangels: Azrael, Chamuel, Raguel, and Raphael

Associated Chakras: Root, sacral, solar plexus, and heart

Healing Description: Native to Australia, Banksia is a very interesting, unusual flower. It sows its seeds in a unique way: it only opens its seedpods after a fire. Australia is quite a hot, dry country, and prone to bushfires that can destroy many of the plants—except for Banksia. It waits until the temperatures cool down to release its seeds. Thus begins new life from the ashes. This flower brings this same energy to you. It picks you back up after you feel you cannot possibly go forward.

Message from Banksia: "When you're at the end of your rope, I'll give you the spark of life, which will reignite your passion and take you back to the path of love and light. Let's leave behind all the cares and concerns of the past, and let's release all old toxins and heavy energies. Then you will be able to rise from the ashes surrounding you now. You're a beautiful being and a child of God. Please allow yourself to take this second chance—you deserve it! Don't buy into the thoughts and feelings from the past that were telling you that your aspirations are turned to dust. Let me pick you up so you can gently recharge. I'll help you take the first step in this new phase of your life."

Begonia

Botanical Name: *Begonia* spp.

Energetic Properties: Removing irritation, releasing anger, clearing frustration, promoting patience and calmness, and setting boundaries

Associated Archangel: Raphael

Associated Chakras: Root, sacral, and solar plexus

Healing Description: Begonia reminds you of the importance of patience and is willing to help you for as long as you need it. It guides you along the path of calm and peace. This flower helps you retain your personal space and free yourself from distractions. It prevents others from entering your area, because these people often prevent you from working.

Message from Begonia: "Please allow me to bring you what you need at this time: patience and calm. You'll soon realize that lack of patience underlies any lower emotions you're feeling. Allow me to remind you of this and help you feel it fully. Patience is a big lesson to learn, so I'll stay with you for the duration.

"When you keep finding others in your personal space, I'll set up some etheric boundaries to shield you. However, let's take a moment to look at why people keep coming into your space. Some may say that it's because you haven't been strict enough, but I'll tell you the true reason: they're attracted to you and your energy. You have a wonderful aura, and people feel this tranquility when they interact with you. I will help you safely share your healing gifts with others while protecting yourself."

Bird-of-Paradise

Alternative Name: Crane flower

Botanical Name: *Strelitzia* spp.

Energetic Properties: Enhancing communication, connecting to the angels and deceased loved ones, clearing chakras, and helping to give psychic readings or speeches

Associated Archangels: Gabriel and Metatron

Associated Chakras: Throat, third eye, and crown

Healing Description: Bird-of-Paradise is a flower of communication and spirituality. It heightens your vibration and brings you to the same level as the angels. It releases all blockages you had, making it easy to communicate with these beings of love and light. This makes it a wonderful flower for psychics and angel readers; have some Bird-of-Paradise flowers nearby while you do your healing work. They're also great to keep close when you're onstage or giving live group readings because they keep your energy high and your connection to the angels strong and pure.

Message from Bird-of-Paradise: "I'll ease you through any blockages of communication. I'll clear the path to higher realms and tune you in to the spiritual connections that are right there waiting for you. I help open up channels so you can convey loving messages to others. Experience my vibration. You'll find that you're able to connect with your angels and communicate with them effortlessly. I cleanse and balance all your chakras and energy centers to make your communication even easier. Your intuition will be taken to higher levels of accuracy. I encourage you to trust and act upon your feelings."

Black-eyed Susan

Botanical Name: *Rudbeckia hirta*

Energetic Properties: Releasing old emotions and toxins, healing past relationships, lifting depression, increasing self-esteem, and cutting ties to the past

Associated Archangels: Jeremiel, Raphael, Raziel, and Sandalphon

Associated Chakras: Solar plexus and heart

Healing Description: Black-eyed Susan helps release negative energy from the past. It tells you it's time to banish baggage and move forward into your future. Free yourself from the old emotions and heaviness. Black-eyed Susan helps correct your past relationships so that your future ones can be beautiful, two-way exchanges of energy that involve equally giving and receiving love. You will notice the profound difference this process of releasing has on your body.

Message from Black-eyed Susan: "It's now time for you to release the pain you've held on to. Be willing to rid your body of toxins and negativity; exchange them for peace and love. You'll feel instantly lighter. You're saying to the Universe that you're no longer willing to let the past control your life, and you're ready to move forward. Let go and make more room for love in your life. Love is a two-way street, yet your relationship history has been more like a *one*-way street. You were exhausting yourself by giving, giving, giving; and it just left you feeling tired at the end. You deserve to *be* loved just as much as you *give* love."

Bleeding Heart

Alternative Names: Venus's car and lyre flower

Botanical Name: *Lamprocapnos spectabilis*

Energetic Properties: Heart healing; releasing old pain, heavy emotions, and resentment; and bringing about forgiveness

Associated Archangels: Jophiel and Raphael

Associated Chakra: Heart

Healing Description: Bleeding Heart's blossoms clear old, painful emotions (such as resentment) and bring lightness to the whole situation. The energy of Bleeding Heart is gentle and comforting. It never pushes or forces you into the healing process; instead, it shows what it would be like to choose the path of peace. When you opt to release heaviness from your life, you will be exposed to the true light of the angels.

Message from Bleeding Heart: "I'm here so you can gently open up your heart to the healing light of the angels, who are bringing love toward you at every moment. I can see deep within your heart and know that you are burdened by the energy of hurtful memories and emotions. I can help you heal and release them once and for all. Please be honest with yourself. Don't judge yourself or others. Instead, focus on love: the love that the angels have for you, that God carries for you, and that which lies in your heart. Lift the veil of old emotions and see how much love and joy there is. Now is the time to let go of the past and claim your positive future.

"Let me guide you through a very gentle healing method: Take several deep breaths and relax. Focus on my image. You'll soon feel my warm, heartfelt embrace. Know that I'm here to lift this old hurt from you. Imagine yourself feeling good and confident once again. Allow your body and mind to release these past events; let them go as quickly as they flash through your mind. Feel the healing warmth that I'm bringing to your heart and chest. Dissolve the heaviness, and leave behind only love."

Bluebell

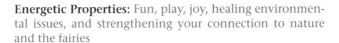

Alternative Names: English bluebell and common bluebell

Botanical Name: *Hyacinthoides non-scripta*

Energetic Properties: Fun, play, joy, healing environmental issues, and strengthening your connection to nature and the fairies

Associated Archangel: Ariel

Associated Chakras: Sacral and solar plexus

Healing Description: Bluebells are protective of nature and can help heal any kind of environmental concerns, as they are very connected to Mother Earth and have a strong affinity to the fairies. Like the fairies, Bluebells have two sides to them: a fun, joyous side and a serious one. The more you work with this flower, the more laughter and happiness you'll find in your life, with a strong undercurrent of playfulness. Your emotions and thoughts will be lifted to greater heights of joy. The fairies know that many people have little time for fun, so they're passionate about opening doors allowing you to play.

Message from Bluebell: "Fun! I bring happiness and lightness to your spirit. I'm very much connected to the energy of the fairies; I work closely with them and help them. Often I provide a haven for these wonderful nature spirits. Imagine how lucky I feel when a fairy entrusts me with sheltering it for the night. When working with me, you'll feel the uplifting energy that fairies bring you. You may find that you become sensitive to nature-based topics and discover a newfound passion for Mother Earth. Please indulge any urges to spend more time outdoors. I'll reward you with love and happiness."

Bottlebrush

Botanical Name: *Callistemon* spp.

Energetic Properties: Increasing motivation, connecting to your passion, and detoxification

Associated Archangels: Metatron, Michael, and Raphael

Associated Chakras: Sacral, solar plexus, heart, and crown

Healing Description: Bottlebrush helps locate the part of you that you feel is missing—but in truth, you're perfectly whole. This flower reminds you to look at the true form of your being. When you do so, your passion and motivation get a huge overhaul. You'll feel excited about completing tasks that you've put off, and you'll get many things done in one day that would previously have taken you weeks to complete. Bottlebrush also reminds you to enjoy this newfound drive and ensure that it continues by nurturing your physical body.

Message from Bottlebrush: "Please allow me to increase your motivation and your zest for life. I can reignite the spark of passion that lies within you. I'll help you reconnect to the happiness and drive you once had. You've slipped a little, and this is okay. Please don't judge yourself or put yourself down. You're beautiful, and just as perfect as the day you were born. There's nothing that you need to change about yourself. Instead, I encourage you to lift this heaviness that surrounds you. Please be willing to embrace this exciting change. It will gently coax you through the tough times and bring you out the other side into the sunshine. You'll be able to find your passion, and lift yourself out of this slump to experience fun again.

"One way to start is by clearing out all toxins. Please don't jump into this on your own; it's best to have support from those who know what they're doing, such as a healthcare practitioner or naturopath."

Bougainvillea

Alternative Name: Paper flower

Botanical Name: *Bougainvillea* spp.

Energetic Property: Protection

Associated Archangel: Michael

Associated Chakra: Root

Healing Description: Contrary to what you might think, the flower of the Bougainvillea is actually the small, almost insignificant white blossoms. The colored leaves that look like petals are called *bracts,* and they aren't flowers at all. This is talking botanically—energetically, it's another story. The leaves act as protective forces around the small flower.

Bougainvillea vines are excellent to plant along fences. They prevent lower energy from entering your property, and keep you and your family protected. Envisioning your home completely surrounded by Bougainvillea is a powerful means of shielding against lower energy.

Message from Bougainvillea: "I'm here to protect you from all undesirable things—in the physical as well as the spiritual world. I'll form a shield around you, your loved ones, and home. I act like a barrier to negativity of all kinds. When you're feeling small and weak, I'll give you strength. Here is the courage to stand up and be proud; you have nothing to fear. It's time for you to step forward boldly. Your Divine light never fades; it continues to shine as brightly as it always has. I will protect you while you take down your walls. Together, let's expose your true Divine beauty."

Bromeliad

Alternative Names: Vase plant and urn plant

Botanical Name: *Aechmea* spp., *Guzmania* spp., *Neoregelia* spp., *Tillandsia* spp., and *Vriesia* spp.

Energetic Properties: Clearing negative thinking, bringing your focus to the positive, assuring you of Heaven's help, and connecting you to God

Associated Archangels: Michael and Sandalphon

Associated Chakras: Third eye and crown

Healing Description: The energy of Bromeliad is wonderful to experience. It reminds you that Heaven is always watching over you. A moment never passes when you are alone; you are always cared for. Bromeliad reminds you that you never need to go down the darker path. You will always find a kind and gentle friend to walk you down the path of light, whether this friend is physical or Divine. When you work with Bromeliad, your thoughts become more balanced, and you focus more on the positive in every situation. No longer will you allow yourself to drift into doubt and despair; instead, you remain focused on the higher vibration of love and light.

Message from Bromeliad: "I want to remove the negativity you're experiencing. Allow me to take away those feelings that something bad is on the horizon. I can hear those constant thoughts of doubt; you're feeling that if life is going too well, 'it just can't be this good.' You question whether Heaven is really listening or cares. Allow me to open up your crown chakra and connect you to God, the true and ultimate source of love. Feel this Divine connection to Spirit, and notice all your concerns lift from your body and dissolve in the light. Know that you deserve the best that life has to offer, and focus on the optimal outcome in every situation. At each moment, God is helping, guiding, and supporting you in every way."

Cactus

Botanical Name: Any from the *Cactaceae* family

Energetic Properties: Protection, time to heal, removing feelings of being fragile, balancing your sensitivity, and spiritual growth

Associated Archangels: Metatron, Michael, Raphael, and Raziel

Associated Chakras: Solar plexus, heart, third eye, and crown

Healing Description: The flowers that bloom on a Cactus plant are strikingly beautiful. The only shame is that they never last long enough! Cacti show that we must never judge a book by its cover: although these succulents can be spiny and prickly, they can produce healing flowers that are breathtaking.

The flowers urge you to take the space and time you need to nurture your body and spirit. This protection is helpful while you adjust to your increasing sensitivity to energy. The flowers of the Cactus want to help you and make you feel as comfortable as possible during this time. Think of them like a mother bear: they will protect you from danger and keep you safe and warm while you grow.

Message from Cactus: "Allow me to protect you while you're feeling vulnerable. I know that you're more sensitive than normal. I've noticed your emotions going up and down. It's okay; I will form a protective shield around you so you have the space you need to heal and grow. Remember to nurture your soul while you regain your strength. You needn't judge yourself for how you're feeling; it's all part of the stage of growth that you're going through. You're moving toward a more intuitive and energetic way of being. These ups and downs are like growing pains. You're experiencing scattered emotions because you're not sure how to handle them right now, but I'm here to gently teach you so you may become more spiritual."

Calendula

Alternative Name: Pot marigold

Botanical Name: *Calendula officinalis*

Energetic Properties: Healing, aura strengthening and repair, lifting emotions, and enhancing joy

Associated Archangel: Raphael

Associated Chakras: Solar plexus and heart

Healing Description: Calendula is primarily a healing flower, assisting you with physical, mental, and energetic concerns. It will help you find the best practitioner or therapy, bringing you the most effective healing safely and gently. Calendula repairs your aura, provides strength to your auric shield, and works wonders on your mental and emotional states.

Message from Calendula: "I'm the healer. I direct all kinds of positive energy toward you. I'll guide you to the perfect method of moving through this health concern. I have a particular affinity for healing the aura, and I will repair and strengthen yours. I can make your energetic field a strong, protective barrier around you so that only loving energies may enter, and lower vibrations are kept at bay.

"I lift your emotions and heal the mind and spirit. Enjoy the lightness and laughter that I'm bringing you now. You'll find that your self-esteem, self-confidence, and natural energy levels will rise. Feel your vitality increase through me."

Calla Lily

Alternative Names: Arum lily, Easter lily, and calla

Botanical Name: *Zantedeschia aethiopica*

Energetic Properties: Attracting and enhancing romantic relationships, saying "I love you" to your soul mate, and healing grief

Associated Archangel: Jophiel

Associated Chakra: Heart

Healing Description: Calla Lily helps enhance your relationship with your soul mate. It acts as an attractor, like a moth to a flame. Your meeting will come easily and with perfect Divine timing.

Calla Lilies can be used for both weddings and funerals, because their energetic message says, "I love you."

Message from Calla Lily: "I carry with me the energy of your soul mate and can help you both by strengthening your bond. If you have yet to encounter the right person, I can bring your paths together so that you meet in the most perfect and romantic way. You will find a true love connection, and your relationship will grow and blossom in the right amount of time. Once you've found each other, I ensure that your love never wavers. Even if your soul mate crosses the veil into the afterlife, I keep your feelings connected in the energy of love. I will help you move through your grief by reminding you of the emotions and good times you shared."

Camellia

Botanical Name: *Camellia* spp.

Energetic Properties: Finding your perfect match, finding yourself, and overcoming loss

Associated Archangels: Chamuel, Jeremiel, Jophiel, and Raphael

Associated Chakras: Sacral, solar plexus, heart, and crown

Healing Description: Camellia flowers help attract more love into your life: the authentic love that you deserve and crave. When seeking a romantic partner, this flower can help manifest your perfect match in two ways. First, it reminds you of who you truly are and what you want in a partner. Then it serves as a magnet to this person, drawing him or her closer to you day by day. If you're already in a loving relationship, this flower signals that it's time to reconnect and to be more conscious of the true love and passion that you share. It reminds you of what you love about each other, then takes your relationship to the next level.

Camellia can help release lower emotions, which may be lodged in your heart. Have you or someone you know been in mourning for a long time; for example, feeling like you've "never been the same" since you lost a loved one? This is the perfect flower for these situations.

Message from Camellia: "I can help dissolve heavier emotions from your past that may still affect you, including grief and loss (perhaps from previous relationships or departed loved ones). I'm here to serve as a reminder that you're very much loved. Feel the love from your dear ones on the other side, holding you in a comforting embrace.

"I'll also help you find yourself. It's time for you to accept yourself for who you truly are. Then allow me to bring you love! I'll help search for your perfect match, a loving relationship with someone who will fully accept you. There's no need for you to pretend; accept who you really are. Becoming comfortable with yourself allows me to bring you the person best suited to the *true* you. Previously, you might have felt you had to act in certain ways to deserve love, but this has never been the case. Please release these views, and get ready for your new romance!"

Carnation

Alternative Names: Pinks and gillyflower

Botanical Name: *Dianthus caryophyllus*

Energetic Properties: Faithfulness, commitment, and attracting soul-mate relationships

Associated Archangels: Haniel and Jophiel

Associated Chakras: Root and heart

Healing Description: Carnations are wonderful relationship flowers. They ensure that things always work out positively, and that both partners are equally invested. It's a lovely idea to have Carnations at weddings. This promotes long-lasting, loyal relationships in which both parties find mutual fulfillment. This flower also helps attract soul mates for those who have not yet found them.

Message from Carnation: "I'm here to help with fidelity. When you're surrounded by my energy, there will be no doubts about your faithfulness. You'll never have a wandering eye when you're close to me. I ensure that your relationship is honest and loving and that one partner isn't keeping secrets from the other. I gently coax out the truth and bring situations into the light for healing.

"If you're looking for your soul mate, I will help. I'll give clear proof that this person is your true partner, and there will be no doubts in your mind. I'll help you release any fears of commitment. Let go of anxieties so that you truly honor your feelings. Enjoy this love that you truly deserve. If you receive guidance that this romantic partner isn't right for you, please honor this. I'll help you gracefully go your separate ways. In your soul-mate relationship, I'll bring love and strengthen the pure bond between you."

Cherry Blossom

Botanical Name: *Prunus* spp.

Common Variety: Japanese cherry (*Prunus serrulata*)

Energetic Properties: Enhancing romance; strengthening relationships; finding out the true intentions of your partner; grace, poise, civility, and taking the high road

Associated Archangels: Haniel and Jophiel

Associated Chakra: Heart

Healing Description: Cherry Blossoms bring romance and grace. They ensure you're always relaxed and speak clearly, with heartfelt intentions. There's no need for you to bring your own energy down. It's more important to stay true to yourself. When working with this flower, you'll always act authentically.

Cherry trees are wonderful meeting places for potential romances. They let you see the true potential for the relationship and also allow you to relax and enjoy the experience. You can plant a cherry tree in your own backyard to protect you from partnerships that aren't for your highest good.

Message from Cherry Blossom: "You know that there's no need to act inappropriately or childish. Together we can rise above this current situation, not add to the drama and heavy energy that surrounds it. You'll always act like a perfect gentleman or lady. I can assist you in always behaving appropriately and calmly, yet with heartfelt emotion."

Chrysanthemum

Alternative Name: Mum

Botanical Name: *Chrysanthemum indicum*

Energetic Properties: Enhancing familial bonds, healing sibling rivalry, and allowing members of a household to get along

Associated Archangels: Chamuel and Raguel

Associated Chakras: Root, solar plexus, and heart

Healing Description: A Chrysanthemum is like a nice, warm, comforting hug. It brings unity within homes so that everybody living under one roof can cohabitate in peace. It releases the ego mind-sets of jealousy and rivalry. Chrysanthemum is useful when there are people who don't get along. The flower helps bring balance so there are no squabbles, just more fun. This is a great choice to incorporate into the decor when hosting dinner parties and get-togethers.

Message from Chrysanthemum: "I'll help bring your family closer and heal any rifts within the group. Soon your family will be closer than ever, coexisting harmoniously and lovingly. This is what makes God and the angels the happiest. Allow me to clear any kind of jealousy; let me remove sibling rivalry. I want to remind everyone of the fun and love they share . . . and crave from one another. I love working with families. I can help any household that's unbalanced or dysfunctional."

Clover

Alternative Name: Shamrock

Botanical Name: *Trifolium* spp.

Common Varieties: White or Dutch clover (*Trifolium repens*) and red clover (*Trifolium pretense*)

Energetic Properties: Perseverance, remembering to ask for help, going forward, attracting money, and fulfillment of financial goals

Associated Archangels: Jeremiel, Raziel, and Uriel

Associated Chakras: Root, heart, and crown

Healing Description: People tend to focus on the leaves of the green clover, connecting to the old associations and images of shamrocks. Here we focus instead on the Clover flower. Clover grows as a weed in many countries, making it easily accessible for most people. The flowers make powerful healing garlands that help you move forward in your current situation and attract financial security. The closer you're able to keep this flower to you, the better. Carry one of its blossoms in your pocket, or bag so it can help you throughout the day.

You can also try creating a very simple Clover chain: First, gather a few dozen Clover flowers. Carefully make a cut at the end of each stem, similar to the eye of a sewing needle—it's easy to do using just a fingernail. Thread the stem of one flower through the hole in the next flower's stem. Continue linking flowers in this way until you have a long, magical chain of abundance.

Message from Clover: "Although I'm a simple flower, I bring the energy of perseverance. When the going gets tough, I help you continue moving forward. You can move through the difficult times, but there's no need to push ahead on your own; call upon others for assistance. Aid may come from your angels when you give them permission and invite them into your life.

"I can help with your financial dreams and bring wonderful prosperity right now. You'll no longer feel as if that magical pot of gold is always out of reach; I'll bring it within easy grasp. Now is your time. I know that you've been trying hard, and I want to reward your dedication."

Crab Apple

Botanical Name: *Malus* spp.

Energetic Properties: Trust, going ahead with projects, following guidance, brainstorming new concepts, and sharing your ideas with the world

Associated Archangel: Gabriel

Associated Chakras: Root and sacral

Healing Description: This flower confirms you're on the right path and encourages you to continue. If you have a new idea or are considering a new direction, Crab Apple gives you the green light to go for it. This flower will help bring together everything you need to move forward with your concept. The main theme of Crab Apple is trust: you are asked to have faith in the guidance that you've been given. It won't be long until your idea is ready to be shared with the world. Congratulations!

Message from Crab Apple: "Trust in your new idea, as it is no ordinary one; rather, it's Divine inspiration from God and the angels. I'm here to confirm this for you, and assure you that you're making the right decision. I'll guide you as you move forward with this idea. It may take time to come to fruition, so please be patient. I will bring you the tools, people, and money you need. Just like a bird hatching from an egg, you're ready to break through your walls. Show the world the beautiful idea you're bringing into it."

Crocus

Botanical Name: *Crocus* spp.

Energetic Properties: Enhancing your abilities as a spiritual teacher and giving you the courage to begin teaching

Associated Archangel: Raziel

Associated Chakras: Third eye and crown

Healing Description: The Crocus gives you confidence and courage. It helps you take a leap of faith as you fulfill your purpose as a spiritual teacher. This flower knows that you've been putting off following your life path. You might reinterpret the intuitive messages that you're given because you're letting fear take control. Fear is preventing you from teaching others what you love, but guess what . . . You've already been teaching! Whenever you speak about spirituality, people are learning from you. What seems like common knowledge to you is a profound awakening to someone else. Now it's time for you to take the next step. Accept your purpose as a wonderful spiritual teacher and continue to *inspire.*

Message from Crocus: "You're a spiritual teacher. Please don't look for further confirmation of this. I urge you to take this message to heart. Now is the time for you to begin. You have so much wisdom and love to convey to others. You needn't start with huge classes; teaching one person is enough. Then the flow of energy will begin moving.

"Accept your God-given abilities. Take the leap; the angels support you through this magical adventure. What a wonderful journey you're embarking on! There are many blessings in store for you and others. Please don't feel that you're not ready or that you don't have enough training. You have everything you need to begin making a real difference in the lives of others. Begin sharing your Divine knowledge with those around you, and I will bring you all the students you can take on easily. Remember to remain humble and grounded. Everyone has the same opportunities, and no one is better than the next person. It is so gratifying to see you take this step forward!"

Daffodil

Alternative Names: Lent lily and narcissus

Botanical Name: *Narcissus* spp.

Energetic Properties: Opening up communication channels, assisting with writing and speeches, and bringing projects to completion

Associated Archangels: Gabriel, Michael, and Raphael

Associated Chakras: Throat, heart, and third eye

Healing Description: Daffodil is the chief flower of communication and is very connected to Archangel Gabriel. It supports you in completing assignments with gentle ease. Its energy helps with all forms of communication, whether spoken or written, and reminds you to phrase everything in a loving, positive way. When you give speeches, Daffodil brings confidence and helps open up your audience so they're willing to receive your messages. Daffodil can also help children and adults who have difficulties with speech.

Message from Daffodil: "Invite me into your life and your communication will be balanced and Divinely guided. I will build a filter over your throat chakra so that every word that passes your lips is filled with love. I also assist children who have learning disabilities or speech impediments in a gentle and comforting way. They'll feel happy within themselves again and never buy into others' negative judgments.

"I will help you always be composed and confident during speaking events so that you can deliver your Divine message to those who need to hear it. I can also be a wonderful muse for your writing. I'll guide you to stick to a schedule and complete every project you undertake. I'll give everything you do the energy of love and peace."

Dahlia

Botanical Name: *Dahlia* spp.

Energetic Properties: Empowerment and reminding you that one person can make a difference

Associated Archangels: Michael and Zadkiel

Associated Chakras: Root and crown

Healing Description: Dahlia reminds you that you are powerful and only *you* can fulfill your life purpose. Realize that being powerful doesn't mean being pushy, forceful, or threatening. You can make positive life changes by being assertive and in balance. Dahlia encourages you to follow your inner guidance. Remember that the energy of the angels is loving and peaceful, while the ego is heavy and overpowering.

Message from Dahlia: "Yes, you *can* make a real difference! You have an amazing light within you; please fully accept it so that others can enjoy your beauty. Everyone has a life purpose, and it's time for you to acknowledge yours. You're the only person who can complete your mission, and the angels will guide you each step of the way. They'll ensure that you never waver from your path.

"When you accept your power, you can make a difference in the lives of those around you. Remember the adage, 'Lead by example'? If you're walking the path of peace, others will notice and reflect peace as well. You're powerful in a loving way. Now it's time for you to start occupying the role you were put on this planet to fulfill. Change your current situation . . . and the world."

Daisy

Alternative Names: Common daisy, lawn daisy, and English daisy

Botanical Name: *Bellis perennis*

Energetic Properties: Removing drama and stress, simplifying your life, relaxation, and self-care

Associated Archangel: Metatron

Associated Chakras: Root, sacral, solar plexus, and crown

Healing Description: If Daisies surround you or you feel drawn to this page, please take note. Give yourself some time to relax and recharge your batteries. The angels understand that you've had quite a lot on your plate recently, and they're embracing you now. Let them take care of you and lift the stress from your shoulders. Think of a child making Daisy chains: this is the state of mind that this flower brings into your life. Daisies deliver peace to your life so you can focus on what is important.

Message from Daisy: "You need to simplify! You've got so much going on, and you're spread too thin. Your energy levels are dropping, and you're becoming tired more easily. This has to stop now! I'm surrounding you, and giving you the opportunity to take away the drama and stress. Let me help you heal this situation so you can be focused and relaxed at all times. You may think relaxation is not an option for you, but you must make it part of your daily routine. I urge you to find methods of self-care and spend a moment each day doing something you love—reading, meditating, gardening, or anything that brings you relief. Rest assured that your stress is leaving; I'm working with you now to make this happen."

Dandelion

Botanical Name: *Taraxacum officinale*

Energetic Properties: Releasing lower energies, teaching you how to handle emotions, and granting wishes

Associated Archangels: Jophiel, Raguel, Raphael, and Raziel

Associated Chakras: Root, heart, throat, and crown

Healing Description: Dandelion has several applications. The yellow flower can heal anger, resentment, bitterness, and jealousy. It doesn't take away these lower emotions; instead, it brings to your attention the reasons why you have them. Then you can understand these emotions and be better able to deal with similar experiences in the future. The characteristic white, snowball-like Dandelion seeds are great to work with; they're especially good for making your dreams come true. Try this manifestation technique, familiar to most children: Pick a "snowball" and hold the stem in your hands. Close your eyes for a moment, and take a few deep breaths. Focus on your desires and your true heartfelt goals. See them as real right now! Take two slow, deep breaths; then, as you take a third breath, open your eyes and blow with all your might, sending the seeds into the air. The angels say they're like little messengers that go out, completing your request.

Message from Dandelion: "Remember to ask for help from the angels. They can rush to your side, providing you with the relief and love you need. I'd like to help you rise above lower-energy emotions like bitterness and anger. Once you analyze them, you can acknowledge their true cause, then remove and release it. Getting mad is the result of emotions being channeled incorrectly—when your body is unsure of how to interpret the feelings that it's experiencing, it processes them as anger. Look at your current situation: are you truly frustrated and angry with others . . . or with yourself?

"I can also help with manifesting your wishes. Let's bring your heart's true desires into your physical reality."

Delphinium

Alternative Name: Larkspur

Botanical Name: *Delphinium* spp.

Common Variety: Candle larkspur (*Delphinium elatum*)

Energetic Properties: Achieving your desires, taking charge, positive transitions, trusting in Divine assistance, and protection while in the ocean

Associated Archangels: Michael and Sandalphon

Associated Chakras: Root, sacral, solar plexus, third eye, and crown

Healing Description: Delphinium releases any doubts you might have about your next steps. It pushes you in the right direction and reminds you that you're strong enough to carry on. More important, Delphinium reminds you to trust that you are Divinely guided and supported. The angels and flowers will guide you through these transitions. Everything will work out for your highest good when you trust.

Delphinium also has a connection to the ocean. Its name is derived from the Greek word for *dolphin*, due to the petals' resemblance to the nose of the bottlenose variety. It helps protect you when you're in the ocean and is especially useful if you're constantly diving and swimming.

Message from Delphinium: "I ask you to reach for the stars! There's nothing standing in your way. You're strong enough to move forward. You have the power to achieve the great things you've been contemplating, and I'm here to tell you that it's time to stop thinking, and start *doing* them. Release the fear, and enjoy the exciting new adventure you're about to embark upon. You've been climbing ever higher, but it's now time for me to speed things up a little. I understand that you may feel overwhelmed, but fear not. When you trust in me and the angels, you'll find amazing gifts coming at incredible speeds.

"My strong connection to the ocean makes me useful for those living close to large bodies of water. I protect anyone who enjoys swimming and diving regularly. I serve to safeguard you while you're immersed in water, and ensure that you have magical and healing experiences."

Dianthus

Botanical Name: *Dianthus* spp.

Common Variety: Sweet William (*Dianthus barbatus*)

Energetic Properties: Attracting joy, love, and romance; manifestation; granting wishes; reminding you to play; and an all-purpose flower

Associated Archangels: Gabriel, Jophiel, Metatron, Michael, Raphael, and Uriel

Associated Chakras: All chakras

Healing Description: When you connect with this flower, you'll enjoy many fun experiences. Surrounded with loving people, you open up your heart. Dianthus allows you to attract and connect with your true desires, and guides you in your steps toward achieving them. This flower helps you find joy within yourself. In this way, you set a beautiful example for others; then they, too, begin to heal and will eventually join you.

Dianthus is also a go-to flower for *any* concerns you may have. You can easily work with it if you cannot find the perfect flower for your situation.

Message from Dianthus: "I bring you joy, love, and upbeat energy. Play should always be at the top of your list! I'll help manifest your heart's desires, and comfort you in your time of need. Call on me; I can guide you in many different ways. If you ask, I will collaborate closely with the angelic realm so that we're all working toward your highest good.

"Get ready, because we're about to embark on a very fun and uplifting journey! Now is the time for you to be truly happy. There's no reason why you cannot have everything your heart longs for, so let's fill your life with love and joy. I'll bring you to a perfect state of peace, and you will inspire others to come on this magical journey with you."

Echinacea

Alternative Name: Purple cone-flower

Botanical Name: *Echinacea* spp.

Energetic Properties: Opening your third eye, enhancing clairvoyance, and clearing fear

Associated Archangel: Michael

Associated Chakra: Third eye

Healing Description: Echinacea is well known for its ability to stimulate the immune system. It has a cleansing effect on not only the physical body, but also the energetic one. Echinacea has a strong affinity with the third-eye chakra, which is your center of psychic visions and clairvoyance. It will remove any fears you might have so that you can fully enjoy your God-given abilities. You'll notice your spirituality deepening as you continue working with Echinacea flowers.

The root of Echinacea is medicinal. You can make a tea from it—a tasty way to enhance your clairvoyance.

Message from Echinacea: "I'll clear away blocks you might have to fully accepting your Divine spiritual and psychic abilities. These are your birthright; they are yours to use. I know that you have some fear-based thoughts about your third-eye chakra, but there's no need for concern. Perhaps you think you'll be given frightening information once you open up this chakra. However, rest assured that I'll prevent that from happening. Your angels have only loving and supportive messages to give you. Open the floodgates to clairvoyance: you will be filled with love and joy."

Eucalyptus

Alternative Names: Eucalypt and gum tree

Botanical Name: *Eucalyptus* spp.

Energetic Properties: Blessings, attracting miracles, granting permission for your angels to help you, and removing barriers to receiving

Associated Archangels: Metatron, Michael, Raphael, and Raziel

Associated Chakras: Root, throat, third eye, and crown

Healing Description: Eucalyptus is a flower of receiving. It reminds you that sometimes, even though help may be right around you, you must ask for it. This flower will bring many amazing changes to your life. You most definitely deserve these blessings. Please open your arms and heart wide with the energy of Eucalyptus.

Message from Eucalyptus: "I'll work with you to gently open up your heart so that you are fully willing to receive blessings. Please accept the love that you so richly deserve. The angels are by your side at every moment of every day, as am I. Remember that the Law of Free Will prevents you from receiving blessings and healing until you give permission. Once you declare to the Universe that you're ready and willing to receive, your loving angels and I can help. Allow yourself to flow into this receptive state and you'll quickly notice miracles begin to happen around you. When you open up to receiving, your life becomes so much easier. God and the angels will personally deliver everything you need. They'll help you function at your best. Amazing opportunities will fall into your lap, and you will receive them in wonder, making you feel happier, healthier, and loved."

Forget-me-not

Botanical Name: *Myosotis* spp.

Energetic Properties: Past-life issues, healing trauma, and connecting to the stars and other planets

Associated Archangel: Raziel

Associated Chakras: Third eye and crown

Healing Description: Forget-me-not helps you remember your past lives, which can give you clues about your current way of living. They provide insight into your relationships and help you find patterns in your chosen career path. You'll often be taken on a very profound journey. Accept only the lessons and love from the past; let go of the rest, including guilt and other emotions that will not serve you. Then you'll be able to move on with your future. Be gentle with yourself during this time of healing. Allow these issues from the past to be released for the highest good of all.

Forget-me-not has a connection to stars and other planets. People who are interested in celestial beings will benefit from the presence of this flower because it may enhance communication with them.

Message from Forget-me-not: "The situations you find yourself in are affected by unresolved issues from your past. Sit with me awhile as we go on a journey back to your previous lifetimes. Here we'll find the moment in which this dysfunctional pattern truly began.

"When you go back to that time, you still remember this current life and the power that you now possess. Learn the origin of your concerns, then bring those lessons back with you to the here-and-now so that you may fully heal them. You're not going on this journey to judge yourself. Release any guilt, and learn from these past situations so you can prevent them from recurring. Let's put an end to negative patterns now."

Frangipani

Alternative Name: Plumeria

Botanical Name: *Plumeria* spp.

Energetic Properties: Spiritual communication, raising your vibration, and enhancing your intuition

Associated Archangels: Metatron and Raziel

Associated Chakras: Third eye and crown

Healing Description: Frangipani helps you elevate your energy, which makes communication with the angels and God a very easy, natural process. Trust in Heaven above. You'll be more deeply connected with your intuition; listen to the feelings and sensations you're being given.

Message from Frangipani: "I'll help you connect even more deeply with the angelic realm. I know that you've desired deeper communication with these beings of love and light who constantly surround you. I'd be honored if you'd allow me to increase your energy levels. I'll raise your vibration to the point where you can clearly hear, see, feel, and know the angels and God. Once this process is complete, you'll have very clear messages and be given constant guidance. Remember to follow your intuitive feelings at every moment."

Freesia

Botanical Name: *Freesia* spp.

Energetic Properties: Healing the spine and back, relieving back tension, finding the perfect health-care practitioner, and bringing strength and courage

Associated Archangels: Michael and Raphael

Associated Chakras: Root and solar plexus

Healing Description: Freesia focuses its energy on the spine by helping with the physical healing of your back, relieving tension or pain. It helps attract the perfect healer and therapist to treat your complaints and nourish your joints. This flower also makes you more aware of your body. You'll start noticing ways in which you can improve your posture, making you feel even more comfortable.

Freesia works on your *energetic* backbone by giving you the courage to stand up for what you believe. It protects you as it allows you to speak your truth. Freesia supports you as you progress spiritually, and makes you feel safe as you grow through self-discovery.

Message from Freesia: "I bring much-needed support to your energetic backbone and give you the courage to show the world who you truly are. I also bring my healing energy to your physical back. Allow it to wrap around your spine and through to your ribs. I'll take away discomfort, and balance areas that are out of alignment. If you've had a history of back issues, consider which healing modalities were most beneficial to you. I'll guide you through this and lead you step-by-step to the ideal therapist for you, someone who will restore your joints to perfect working order."

Fuchsia

Alternative Name: Ladies' ear-drops

Botanical Name: *Fuchsia* spp.

Energetic Properties: Rising above problems, leaving stress behind, and pushing forward

Associated Archangels: Metatron and Michael

Associated Chakras: Root, sacral, solar plexus, and heart

Healing Description: These adorable flowers look like tiny fairies and angels wearing sophisticated robes. The energy of Fuchsia is as uplifting and comforting as a warm hug—very much like that of the angels. This flower allows you to rise above your current situations and concerns, and connect to happiness and a stress-free life. It tells you to keep pressing forward, because you're very close to pushing through and leaving all your obstacles behind.

Message from Fuchsia: "Let me take you by the hand. I'll lift you above where you are and take you to a place of peace and joy. Here you'll be able to fully understand the cause of this current situation. Banish all the tension and stress that you've become accustomed to—this isn't the way to live your life. Please work with me to shed this heaviness. Remember the joy you can experience. Let's take a moment to allow your wings to unfurl so you can soar above your troubles!"

Gardenia

Botanical Name: *Gardenia* spp.

Common Varieties: Cape jasmine (*Gardenia jasminoides*) and tiare or Tahitian gardenia (*Gardenia taitensis*)

Energetic Properties: Releasing stress and worry, encouraging you to have fun, bringing joy and playfulness, and reminding you that your angels are listening to your prayers

Associated Archangels: Metatron, Michael, Raphael, and Sandalphon

Associated Chakras: Root, heart, and crown

Healing Description: Gardenia is excellent for anyone suffering from chronic stress. It's highly recommended that you plant a Gardenia bush in your garden or a large pot—somewhere you can appreciate it regularly. Its flowers clear stressful emotions and remind you that it's time to smile and play. For too long you've had low energy due to the stress surrounding you. Gardenia will make you feel lighter and happier.

Message from Gardenia: "Keep me close, and breathe in my delicate perfume. I'll help you forget about all the stress and worry you once felt. Now it's time for you to enjoy the blissful stage of your life. Gone are the difficult circumstances that were pulling your energy down. Just enjoy each day with a newfound sense of creativity and motivation. Rest assured that the angels have heard your prayers for aid and are helping make things easier right now. Life is meant to be enjoyed and appreciated; there's no reason for you to wake up each day stressed-out. Together let's release your concerns to the angelic realm. You may now enjoy the days ahead."

Geranium

Alternative Name: Cranesbill

Botanical Name: *Geranium* spp.

Energetic Properties: Energetic protection, and strengthening and repairing your aura

Associated Archangels: Metatron, Michael, and Raphael

Associated Chakras: Third eye and crown

Healing Description: Geranium helps heal damage to your auric field. These "breaks" in the aura can be due to a number of things, such as binge drinking, taking illicit drugs, being in negative environments, and being surrounded by negative people. You also damage your aura by forcing yourself to continue with something you have no passion for. Geranium is able to heal all the effects of these situations. However, the energy of this flower cautions you not to abuse its power. Please don't stay in these situations while continually relying on Flower Therapy to clean up the mess.

Message from Geranium: "You've been allowing your energy to expand too far. It's time for you to bring yourself back to center. Let's return your aura to good working order. Your aura was neglected in the past, but now I'm strengthening it so you'll be protected energetically. I can help repair damage that's been done and make your energy field as good as new. Your natural state of vitality and energy will increase, and you'll enjoy each and every day. When you wake up in the morning, you'll jump out of bed, eager to greet the day ahead of you."

Gerbera

Alternative Name: African daisy

Botanical Name: *Gerbera* spp.

Energetic Properties: Comforting old friends, strengthening and balancing relationships, and attracting new friendships

Associated Archangels: Jeremiel and Raguel

Associated Chakras: Sacral, solar plexus, and heart

Healing Description: Gerberas are the perfect flowers to send to friends because they have the ability to solidify your current relationships. You're energetically giving your friends a hug. Send Gerberas when a loved one is in need of comfort and compassion. Gerberas also bring you new and exciting friends who often have a way of helping you. This flower reminds you that friendships don't have to be one-sided. *You* shouldn't be the one constantly giving, listening, and helping. Your friends must be equally compassionate and caring toward you. Gerberas balance this energy flow. They allow your friendships to be mutually enjoyable and rewarding.

Message from Gerbera: "I strengthen and enhance your friendships. I promote unity and peace between friends. Allow me to bring new, true friendships into your life that will give you support and love. If you feel drained, as though your friends are taking advantage of you, allow me to correct this energetic inequality. Let's bring everything back into Divine order. Friendships are about receiving just as much as they are about giving. You deserve to receive!"

Gladiolus

Alternative Name: Sword lily

Botanical Name: *Gladiolus* spp.

Energetic Properties: Raising your energy, increasing happiness, releasing depression, removing grief, and healing heartache

Associated Archangels: Jophiel, Michael, and Raphael

Associated Chakras: Solar plexus and heart

Healing Description: Gladiolus is a magnificent flower, with long stems of deep green and flashes of color from its tower of blossoms. This healing plant releases lower emotions, but this is not a quick fix; it's a step in the right direction. As you lift away the darkness, you expose the light. Shine the light of your being, the light from your soul. It's time to share your inner joy with the world and spread your beauty among others. Gladiolus is perfect for easing heavy emotions and energies such as sadness; this makes it a wonderful gift for a friend in need.

Message from Gladiolus: "I'll lift your spirits in the blink of an eye. Please don't listen to thoughts that tell you enormous amounts of work are ahead. Those voices are the lower vibrations of the ego. I'll help you release them so you can realize the true joy within you right now. You'll feel happy and well again soon. We merely need to peel away the layers of heavy energy that surround you.

This is a simple and easy process, and you'll instantly feel a shift within your body and mind. Enjoy the lightness that I bring. You'll soon forget about those troubling times and emotions, and remember your true state of happiness from this moment on."

Grevillea

Alternative Name: Spider flower

Botanical Name: *Grevillea* spp.

Energetic Properties: Courage to follow your dreams, acceptance of the true you, inspiration in speeches and writing, and men's health

Associated Archangel: Gabriel and Jeremiel

Associated Chakras: Root, throat, and third eye

Healing Description: This flower, which is native to Australia, gently pushes you to continue following your dreams. Grevillea encourages you to feel the fear and do it anyway! Now is your time to grow; no longer can you allow opportunities and guidance to go unnoticed. It's time to share your love with the world, and this flower will help you. Grevillea gives you courage to step out and begin spreading your knowledge. This flower also helps men who are having reproductive concerns.

Message from Grevillea: "It's time for you to trust your intuition and stick your neck out. Release your fears about being the true you, and begin speaking up about what's on your mind. People won't judge you for being yourself. Instead, you'll find that others will appreciate and love you more, and begin communicating with you on an even deeper level.

"You've moved beyond a time when you could sit and watch life pass you by. Now is your time to step up. Find your inner voice and fully accept it as your own. Trust those urges that you've had to give speeches, write books, teach workshops, or attend seminars. Listen, because they are your Divine messages from the angels and me. I'm here to help you take the plunge, so go for it!

"Men with fertility or reproductive concerns should call upon me. I can work on correcting any imbalances and bringing everything back to a perfect state of wellness."

Heather

Alternative Name: Heath, ling, and common heather

Botanical Name: *Calluna vulgaris*

Energetic Property: Bringing calm and healing to pets and all animals

Associated Archangel: Ariel

Associated Chakras: Root, sacral, and heart

Healing Description: Heather aids animals in their times of need. It can bring the kind of therapy that's warranted at this time. Place it near your pet so its healing energy can begin to flow. Your pets will be so appreciative of this generous act of caring.

Message from Heather: "I bring blessings to your animal companions. No matter what their concerns are, I'll help. I'll comfort your pets if they're anxious, settle them into a new home, or soothe their concerns. I bring the healing that your dear animal friends need. None is too big or too small for my energy to help. Add a sprig of me above their beds; mist my essence over their fur, feathers, or scales; or place a photo of me by their favorite spot in order to begin the healing process. Your animals are more than willing to accept this gesture, because they know it's in their best interests to absorb the healing. The energy is pure, and there's no hidden agenda or chemicals that will harm them. I'll bring your friends back to the perfect state of health you know they deserve. And when it's time to let a beloved companion pass, I can help ease the transition into the next world and make the process as gentle and comfortable as possible."

Hibiscus

Alternative Name: Rose mallow

Botanical Name: *Hibiscus* spp.

Common Variety: Shrub Althea,
also known as rose of Sharon (*Hibiscus syriacus*)

Energetic Properties: Unity, togetherness, peace, and happiness

Associated Archangels: Raziel and Chamuel

Associated Chakras: Root, heart, and crown

Healing Description: It's no wonder Hawaiians have long been associated with Hibiscus. This flower's core message is togetherness—the Hawaiian spirit summed up. It reminds you that being in the company of others is far greater than being alone. Yes, one person can make a difference, but that difference can be amplified when surrounded by like-minded people. Hibiscus brings families closer, but the energy goes deeper. It takes you to a soul level, reminding you that we're all from the same Creator and Source.

Message from Hibiscus: "Allow me to bring everyone together. Let me take you to a perfect place of harmony and fellowship. Learn to tune in to that Divine energy of oneness and unity. Imagine yourself, for a moment, feeling perfectly happy and peaceful. Then imagine how this could spread peace through everyone, uniting your family, friends, colleagues, and even people you pass in the street. You have the profound ability to heal them and yourself simply by walking along your personal path of joy and peace. When you are happy, so are those around you. I encourage you to become aware of this connection, and use it so the planet may benefit from your loving energies."

Hyacinth

Alternative Names: Dutch hyacinth, common hyacinth, and garden hyacinth

Botanical Name: *Hyacinthus orientalis*

Energetic Properties: Removing distractions and interruptions, clearing the energy of procrastination, bringing focus and clarity, and freeing up more time

Associated Archangels: Chamuel and Raphael

Associated Chakras: Root and sacral

Healing Description: Use Hyacinth when you feel like you're constantly being interrupted. It can be frustrating when you're kept from completing important work that may lead to your life purpose. It's vital that you have the time and space needed to operate in a cool, calm, collected manner. Hyacinth forms a protective shieldlike energy around your aura to free you from distractions so you can focus on the tasks at hand. This is a great flower for releasing procrastination, a lower energy that tries to prevent us from being the best we can possibly be. Please don't deny yourself any longer. Begin working with Hyacinth to end procrastination once and for all!

Message from Hyacinth: "I help when you have many things on your plate. When you find yourself distracted and interrupted, or you lose the motivation to go on, count on my aid; I'll bring you the focus and clarity you need. I can free up more time for you so you're able to do your work calmly. You never need to feel rushed or overwhelmed. You have endless amounts of time and can do everything you have before you. Take a few deep breaths right now and gaze at me (or my picture). Allow me to help you. Feel my energy surrounding you. I'm forming an energetic barrier between you and your distractions. The angels have big plans for you. I know some tasks don't seem related to your life purpose; however, they need to be completed. Afterward, you'll be presented with the more important tasks in store for you."

Hydrangea

Alternative Name: Hortensia

Botanical Name: *Hydrangea* spp.

Common Varieties: Lacecap or bigleaf hydrangea (*Hydrangea macrophylla*) and PeeGee (*Hydrangea paniculata*)

Energetic Properties: Transformation, life-changing decisions, clearing procrastination, and releasing lower emotions

Associated Archangels: Jeremiel and Sandalphon

Associated Chakras: Root, sacral, and solar plexus

Healing Description: Hydrangeas are remarkable: the color of the blossom is totally dependent on the environment in which the plant is grown and the pH of the soil. This confuses many people who purchase Hydrangeas. Sometimes a person will buy a pink Hydrangea, plant it at home, then discover blue flowers when it blooms the next year. It can certainly seem strange! Just as the blossoms are able to transform themselves into different shades, the energy of Hydrangea brings you the ability to transform yourself. It can be a wondrous helping hand, especially when making life-changing decisions. This flower gently pushes you along in the right direction.

Message from Hydrangea: "I allow for gentle transformation. I can be of immense help when making decisions, especially those that require a complete overhaul in your life. Don't worry; I'll work closely with you to allow this process to happen easily and gradually so you don't experience discomfort during this wonderful transition. I understand that these changes can seem too big or hard, but let's take a moment to look at the first step, which you are able to complete with ease and serenity. Don't focus on the huge mountain in front of you, but rather on each individual step. These amazing, positive life changes can progress at a pace that's comfortable to you. I help you move through lower emotions such as grief and anger, and bring them to a place of love."

Iris

Alternative Names: Fleur-de-lys, flag, and juno

Botanical Name: *Iris* spp.

Energetic Properties: Detoxification, clearing out old energy, and releasing addictions

Associated Archangels: Michael, Raphael, and Uriel

Associated Chakras: Sacral, heart, and crown

Healing Description: The energy of Iris is like a wonderful detox, cleansing your system of old emotions and negativity. You'll feel great after working with it. Your entire body will be recharged, and you'll beam with vitality. Iris can clear away even long-standing aches and pains, as well as any dependencies. Iris encourages a gentle approach that will bring comfort and support during your detoxification period.

Message from Iris: "I will be guiding you to release all things that no longer serve you, such as foods, habits, and addictions. I will also help you release toxins from your body. You will feel refreshed, reenergized, and full of vitality. Notice how you feel better, longer. It may start slowly, but soon you'll realize that you're starting to do more things, even those that you haven't done for a long time."

Jasmine

Botanical Name: *Jasminum* spp.

Common Varieties: Spanish or royal jasmine (*Jasminum grandiflorum*) and common jasmine (*Jasminum officinale*)

Energetic Properties: Peace, deeper meditation, focus on goals, manifestation, and wisdom

Associated Archangel: Raziel

Associated Chakras: Third eye and crown

Healing Description: Jasmine brings a feeling of peace and tranquility. It helps you better concentrate on your highest aspirations. Jasmine also helps you attain more advanced mastery in your contemplative practice, which is one reason why this flower has long been revered by Buddhist monks. The lovely perfume of the blossoms also brings healing.

Message from Jasmine: "I can take you deeper into your meditation experience. Together we can push through any blocks until we connect with your true soul energy: a state of inner peace and well-being. I'll calm your mind and allow you to concentrate. When you connect to my energy, you'll experience a sense of grace and a wonderful calmness that spreads throughout your entire being. You'll be able to focus on your desires and bring them into reality much faster. You'll enjoy an increase in wisdom as I pass down profound spiritual teachings of many generations before you."

Jonquil

Botanical Name: *Narcissus jonquilla*

Energetic Properties: Protecting your energy, healing those around you, bringing more light to your workplace and home, removing harshness from your life, and attracting peaceful environments

Associated Archangels: Jophiel, Metatron, and Michael

Associated Chakras: Third eye and crown

Healing Description: Jonquil blossoms look like miniature daffodils and have a similar energy. This flower, however, focuses upon the people around you and your environment. Jonquil makes surrounding energy more balanced and pure. By working with Jonquils you're able to make a gentle transition into a more peaceful state of being. This may entail distancing yourself from certain people in your life.

Message from Jonquil: "You've been surrounded by people who are too harsh for your sensitive energy to cope with. Call on me, and I'll help heal you and those around you. Some individuals in your life have been acting from the lower energy of the ego. You have considered them friends in the past, but perhaps it's now time to reflect on this. Are you truly willing to continue exposing yourself to this negativity?

"Although this can be a frightening issue, I assure you that the angels are very much with you and gently guiding you to an even better situation. I'll work on healing the voices of those around you so that they too can begin using more loving words and bring more light to the world through their actions. I'll protect your sensitive nature by keeping the energy around you nice and clean. You're strong enough to continue working toward your life purpose."

Lantana

Alternative Name: Shrub verbena

Botanical Name: *Lantana* spp.

Energetic Properties: Increasing love among family members and helping them make decisions together

Associated Archangels: Chamuel, Gabriel, and Raguel

Associated Chakras: Throat and heart

Healing Description: Lantana helps bring families closer together and assists in family communication. It enhances relationships and friendships and gives each individual a voice, especially when trying to come to a big decision. It allows everyone to be happy with the outcome and stand united in the final choice. The essence of Lantana is harmony and unity.

Message from Lantana: "Family togetherness is what I bring for you. I'll ease the channels of communication between you and your loved ones and make sure everyone is getting along perfectly. With Divine intervention, I help you make important choices easily. In decisions that require everyone to be on the same page, such as moving homes or changing jobs, it's important for each person to feel heard. I allow the decision maker to arrive at a firm resolution with love and balance. No one will feel pressured. Allow my healing energy to bring you all closer. The true meaning of my presence is family harmony."

Lavender

Botanical Name: *Lavandula* spp.

Common Varieties: English lavender (*Lavandula angustifolia*) and common lavender (*Lavandula officinalis*)

Energetic Properties: Calming nerves, easing anxieties, promoting sleep, enhancing clairvoyance, and offering comfort and reassurance on your spiritual path

Associated Archangels: Haniel, Jeremiel, Michael, and Raziel

Associated Chakras: Root, solar plexus, and third eye

Healing Description: Lavender is well known for helping soothe the nerves and enhancing sleep. High-quality Lavender essential oil from your local health-food store is a good way to receive this flower's benefits. To prolong the calming, relaxing scent, this flower can be dried and used to fill bags and pillows.

Message from Lavender: "Allow me to hold your hand and give you comfort. There's no reason for you to feel anxious or frightened. I'm here with you now to assure you that all is well. If you place a small bouquet or sachet beside your bed, I will pass on my energetic properties to you all night.

"I also work with your spirituality. I can ease you into greater clairvoyance and enhanced intuition. I'll help release fears you hold about progressing on your spiritual path. Know that your journey is right for you at this time. Please step up to the plate and begin your Divine life mission."

Lilac

Botanical Name: *Syringa vulgaris*

Energetic Properties: Lifting depression, bringing a sense of peace and calmness, releasing anxieties and fears

Associated Archangel: Michael

Associated Chakra: Solar plexus

Healing Description: Lilac is a wonderful calming flower that works to combat the hustle and bustle of everyday life. It is perfect for those with anxiety or depression. When your mood is low, your energy levels are depleted, and each day becomes a huge effort. However, when working with Lilac, you can enjoy each moment of every day. You'll love the new experiences you're able to share with others.

Message from Lilac: "I act like a friend whose warm embrace brings comfort and calmness in your time of need. Relax your mind for a moment. Let's release those irritating, depressing thoughts that were constantly filling your head, and replace them with positive attitudes and feelings. You can do it, and I'm here to support you as you begin to enjoy life in the moment again. There were times in the past when you were feeling down and unhappy, but things are changing at this very moment. You are going to have the life you truly want and deserve. You do not now, nor will you ever, *deserve* to be unhappy and depressed. The angels want you to enjoy each and every day. Please allow me to lift this cloud from you. Then you'll once again be able to experience life's joys."

Lily *(Orange)*

Botanical Name: *Lilium* spp.

Energetic Properties: Lifting depression, building self-esteem, releasing excess baggage, calmness, contentment, and help with weight loss

Associated Archangel: Jophiel

Associated Chakra: Solar plexus

Healing Description: Orange Lilies allow you to look past the small things and enjoy the beauty and joy that's always around you. When stressed, you get caught up in fear energy and lose sight of your many blessings. Orange Lilies help remind you of this and allow you to release old burdens.

If possible, purchase Orange Lilies with closed buds. Sit with them, focus on your intentions for Flower Therapy, and visualize the flowers bursting open. Notice how amazing you feel over the next few days as they slowly blossom, bringing forth your intention and clearing negative emotions. The Lilies can help with depression, low self-esteem, criticism, and even excess weight! They're great to send to friends who are going through a rough patch.

Message from Orange Lily: "I'm going to begin working with you to release your emotional baggage. Let's uncover the person within. I'm here for you. I know that you sometimes have thoughts you don't like, and you've treated yourself poorly in the past. I'd love to help you truly see yourself and love each and every part of your beautiful body. With my help, you'll stop focusing on the small 'imperfections,' and focus instead on all the wonderful things about you. Your so-called imperfections are what make you special and unique. You were created just the way you are for Divine reasons. Whenever you feel low or upset, please call on me, and I'll lift you up to a place of happiness."

Lily (Pink)

Botanical Name: *Lilium* spp.

Energetic Properties: Commitment, promises, and sticking to your decisions

Associated Archangels: Jeremiel and Raziel

Associated Chakras: Sacral and solar plexus

Healing Description: Pink Lilies help you with personal vows, whatever they may be. They're great to use when making pledges to yourself or others, because they ensure that you keep your word. These Lilies also bring reassurance when you are confronted with big decisions. The blooms of the Pink Lily are large and vibrant, serving as a constant reminder of your goals. The deep pink color is a representation of the love and support that comes from your angels and fairies.

Message from Pink Lily: "I can help with all commitments and ensure you don't waver in your resolve. Your commitment may be anything, such as sticking to a healthy eating plan, starting an exercise regime, or focusing more on the love of your angels. Regardless of what you're currently having difficulties with, I'll aid you and give you strength so you can easily accomplish what you desire. Whether it's a written or mental contract with yourself or someone else, I'm here to help."

Lily (Yellow)

Botanical Name: *Lilium* spp.

Energetic Properties: Abundance, prosperity, healing finances, and attracting money

Associated Archangels: Metatron, Michael, and Raphael

Associated Chakras: Root, sacral, and solar plexus

Healing Description: Yellow lilies are of help when you've struggled with your finances. For example, if you need a little more cash for an upcoming vacation, then these Lilies are going to be your best friend. They work intensely to clear away blocks you might have with respect to receiving. Yellow Lilies allow you to attract the abundance you deserve in every aspect of your life. You'll live happily and comfortably, knowing all of your needs are provided for.

Message from Yellow Lily: "When working with me, I'll take care of all your financial concerns. Imagine how nice you'd feel if you didn't have to worry about material matters and all your bills were paid easily. Please give me full access to your financial situation so I can heal any unbalanced relationships you have with money. Take a few deep breaths right now. I act like a magnet, drawing in the energy of abundance from every direction. I attract prosperity in all areas of your life. The hold that money has on you is unhealthy—release this as a thing of the past and eagerly await the abundance I'm sending your way!"

Lily of the Valley

Botanical Name: *Convallaria majalis*

Energetic Properties: Bringing peace, discerning honesty, and awakening you to where you're heading

Associated Archangel: Haniel

Associated Chakra: Crown

Healing Description: This is a sweet flower with a lovely, gentle energy. The peaceful nature of Lily of the Valley will melt away all your concerns. It shows you when someone isn't being completely genuine, so it's perfect when you have concerns about a romantic or business partner. Once you see what he or she is truly out to achieve, you'll be able to move past the situation into a more positive experience. Lily of the Valley also helps you identify your own feelings so that you can be totally honest with yourself, especially about the direction your life is taking.

Message from Lily of the Valley: "Use me to determine the true agenda of those around you. I'll be your personal lie detector, letting you know when people aren't being aboveboard, so that you can quickly remove yourself from inauthentic situations. I'll allow your energy to stay very pure and clean by bringing positive, loving people toward you. I can help with your own agenda by helping you be true yourself; then you'll know whether you're enjoying your current path. Please don't let yourself feel tired. You must ask yourself, 'What am I not accepting in my life purpose?' 'What part of Divine guidance am I not listening to?' and 'What opportunities am I refusing to take?' I'll help pinpoint these issues so you can release them into the light."

Lotus

Alternative Names: Indian lotus and sacred lotus

Botanical Name: *Nelumbo nucifera*

Energetic Properties: Deep spirituality; wisdom; chakra clearing and balancing; and connecting to higher beings, angels, and God

Associated Archangels: Metatron and Raziel

Associated Chakras: All chakras, but primarily crown

Healing Description: The Lotus has a long, rich history steeped in spirituality and wisdom. It assists in deepening and improving your meditation experiences and helps you connect with higher beings for guidance. This blossom is strongly connected to the crown chakra, but is able to cleanse and balance all of your chakras in a gentle and loving way.

Message from Lotus: "I bring profound wisdom. I clear through any blockages you have to achieve your spiritual goals, and guide you to the methods and modalities you will need in order to achieve those goals. I'll help you meditate very deeply, and connect with Divine beings. Let go of any judgments you may have, and let me open you up to a deeper level of growth.

"Sit near a pond full of lotus flowers or hold one between your hands. Close your eyes, breathe deeply, and feel your chakras opening just like one of my blossoms. You can also visualize my petals gently unfurling to reveal the purity of my center."

Magnolia
(Pink)

Botanical Name: *Magnolia* spp.

Energetic Properties: Enhancing fertility and promoting conception

Associated Archangels: Chamuel and Haniel

Associated Chakras: Root, sacral, heart, and crown

Healing Description: The Magnolia is most powerful when it's flowering. Prior to the appearance of the gorgeous blossoms, the bare tree is like a mere skeleton of what it's about to become. Magnolia blossoms soothe concerns and heal difficulties with conception.

Message from Pink Magnolia: "Sit with me; I'll assist you with all aspects of fertility. I am the mother tree. I allow everything to come into balance energetically, which includes aiding conception. Please don't give in to fear. I'm sending you loving angels of fertility. I can work with you whether you're a woman or a man. I love to see couples sitting beneath my blossoms, because I can then bring you both in sync. This is when the true magic occurs. Place one hand on my trunk and the other on your stomach area; notice the sensations and healing energy that I send you."

Magnolia
(White)

Botanical Name: *Magnolia* spp.

Energetic Properties: Removing toxins, clearing pollution and electromagnetic radiation, and releasing addictions

Associated Archangels: Metatron, Michael, and Raphael

Associated Chakra: Sacral

Healing Description: The massive white flowers of the Magnolia are excellent for cleansing physical or energetic toxins from your environment, and especially for ridding the air of cigarette smoke. Magnolia will help if you're looking to rid yourself of any kind of addiction, because it will help you gently and comfortably release harmful substances from your life.

Message from White Magnolia: "If you live near polluted areas or in the heart of a city, I'm a good friend to have. I'll absorb the contaminants from your surroundings so you feel better and clearer. My flowers and dark, glossy leaves bring you healing and help rid you of impurities.

"When you're surrounded by my energy, you'll become more sensitive. Notice if there are certain foods, people, habits, or environments that are now too harsh for you to tolerate. I'm asking you to stop putting yourself and your beautiful body through this discomfort; allow me to help you release impurities for your highest good."

Mandevilla

Botanical Name: *Mandevilla* spp.

Energetic Properties: Dissolving attachments, freedom, room to move, your own space, empowerment, and being yourself

Associated Archangels: Jophiel, Metatron, and Michael

Associated Chakra: Root

Healing Description: The climbing nature of the Mandevilla makes it perfect to plant near a fence. As it grows higher, you'll notice that you, too, are lifted above old situations and regain your sense of independence. The five petals of the flower bring protective energy when you're feeling trapped or when you feel you don't have the freedom to make your own decisions. When you think you can't choose what your heart tells you is best, use Mandevilla to alter the situation! The flowers help you release things that no longer serve you. It is time for you to be your own person and stay true to who you are. Now you can manifest all your desires.

Message from Mandevilla: "I'll release the ties restricting your growth and movement. At times you feel like you're being smothered, and you aren't enjoying the situations in which you find yourself. Fear not; I'm here to help. I'll release your bindings so you may grow and move freely. I hear you've been feeling like you're hitting your head against a brick wall; well, consider it gone. Together we can dissolve all negative attachments. I'll send you forth to create amazing life changes. It's time for you to spread your wings and take flight!"

Marigold

Botanical Name: *Tagetes* spp.

Common Varieties: French marigold (*Tagetes patula*), African marigold (*Tagetes erecta*), and signet marigold (*Tagetes tenuifolia*)

Energetic Properties: Helping you prioritize, bringing clarity and new perspectives, breaking situations into more manageable pieces, moving through blocks, and overcoming obstacles

Associated Archangels: Metatron and Michael

Associated Chakras: Solar plexus, throat, and crown

Healing Description: Use Marigold when you're overwhelmed. It will help you recognize that every daunting task is actually made up of a series of smaller steps. There's nothing you cannot accomplish, and you will soon find it simple to overcome your current difficulties. Move on, step-by-step, until you're past the current situation. Marigold will help you progress with grace and love, and let go of any confusion that's holding you back.

Message from Marigold: "Sometimes situations can seem like overly complicated burdens. Listen to me for a moment, and I'll show you a new way of looking at things. Those seemingly insurmountable obstacles that you're facing aren't as big as you think. They're actually made up of a number of incremental easy-to-achieve steps. Look at my blossoms to give you the inspiration you need. Although one flower may seem like an indistinct clump, when you look closer, I'm nothing more than a collection of petals—just as your situation is no more than a collection of small, manageable steps. I have no doubt you can move past these burdens. You have the strength and willpower to do this, and do it well."

Moonflower

Alternative Name: Moon vine

Botanical Name: *Ipomoea alba*

Energetic Properties: Breaking cycles, getting back on track, and clearing up confusion

Associated Archangels: Jeremiel and Sandalphon

Associated Chakra: Crown

Healing Description: Moon-flower is a vine whose flowers open only at night. It aids you in interrupting cycles or patterns and brings you back to balance in a wholesome way. It helps you quickly learn the lessons involved so you can move through this current state of confusion. Moon-flower gives you 28 days (the duration of the lunar cycle) to return to order.

Message from Moonflower: "Do you feel like you just keep going around in circles? Are you spending weeks trying to come up with an answer, but keep finding yourself back at the beginning? You need to start working with my energy today! I can break the cycle you've slipped into and bring you back into alignment. I'll help you step out of the confusion and see things from a different angle. Give me 28 days, and I'll bring order to your life. You'll be back on your Divine path where you belong."

Nasturtium

Alternative Names: Indian cress and garden nasturtium

Botanical Name: *Tropaeolum majus*

Energetic Properties: Aura strengthening, protection, balancing your finances, attracting abundance, and moderating emotions

Associated Archangels: Metatron and Sandalphon

Associated Chakras: Sacral and solar plexus

Healing Description: Nasturtium brings balance to several areas of your life. It affects your energetic field by shoring up your aura's protective properties. It helps balance your financial situation by keeping you more in tune with the spiritual principles of giving and receiving. (You must be open to receiving, not just giving, in every area of your life.) Nasturtium makes everything lighter and smoother, which helps even out your mood and emotions. You'll be able to enjoy every day to the highest level.

Message from Nasturtium: "I'll help ease the energies surrounding you and increase the size and strength of your aura to protect you from all lower or heavy energy. You'll feel safe and secure as I bring more balance to all areas of your life, including the people around you and your emotions. Please be willing to release any old energy that is slowing you down in your journey toward abundance. You needn't preoccupy yourself with trivial matters. Let go of concerns, especially regarding finances. All things are being taken care of right now. Your prayers have been heard by God and the angels, and they're helping you realize your fullest potential."

Orchid

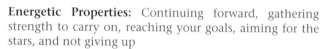

Botanical Name: Any from the *Orchidaceae* family

Common Varieties: *Phalaenopsis* spp., *Dendrobium* spp., *Cymbidium* spp., *Laelia* spp., and *Lycaste* spp.

Energetic Properties: Continuing forward, gathering strength to carry on, reaching your goals, aiming for the stars, and not giving up

Associated Archangels: Jeremiel and Sandalphon

Associated Chakras: Sacral, heart, and crown

Healing Description: The energy of Orchids lifts you up higher and higher. It reminds you that you deserve nothing but the best, and that this is the only thing you should focus on achieving. Orchids act like a support team that keeps pushing you forward even when you feel you can't go on, or when it seems that the reward is too far in the distance.

Message from Orchid: "With each step you take, you're being drawn closer and closer to your goal. Now is not the time to give up; this is the time to push yourself a little further. You'll reap the benefits in the very near future, if you persevere. Continue reaching for the stars. Always focus on your perfect outcome, for this is what you truly deserve. There's no need to focus on, or accept, anything less."

Pansy

Alternative Name: Heartsease

Botanical Name: *Viola tricolor*

Energetic Properties: Enhancing clairvoyance and healing grief

Associated Archangels: Azrael, Metatron, Michael, and Raphael

Associated Chakra: Third eye

Healing Description: This flower opens your third eye, the seat of your clairvoyance. You'll enjoy new experiences when you work with Pansy, such as noticing flashes of light out of the corner of your eye. These are your angels and loved ones sending physical signs that they are with you.

To fully experience this energy, find a single Pansy that you're drawn to. Pick the flower (or purchase it), then lie down on your back. Place the flower facedown on your third eye (this is the area between your two physical eyes). Breathe deeply and become aware of the sensations you experience. You'll feel a slight tingling, and notice that tension has been eased in your forehead.

Message from Pansy: "If you want to see psychically, then you need me! I'll help open up your spiritual sight. You will be able to clearly see the energetic beings that are alongside you, including angels, spirit guides, and deceased loved ones. When you realize that you're always surrounded by heavenly companions, you will heal grief and loss. I'll be with you and do the intensive clearing

146

work on your third-eye chakra. Do not have any doubts concerning the visions and signs you're receiving. Let's journey through a process of awakening your clairvoyance."

Passionflower

Botanical Name: *Passiflora* spp.

Energetic Properties: Feeling the love of your angels; releasing loneliness; bringing comfort and peace; and connecting to your angels, God, and other planets and stars

Associated Archangel: Raziel

Associated Chakras: Heart, third eye, and crown

Healing Description: Passionflower is an exquisite, interesting flower. The blossom looks like the symbol for the crown chakra. It helps open this chakra to allow for better Divine communication, deepening your connection with your angels as well as other planets and star systems (but only with your permission).

The word *passionflower* conjures feelings of romance, which this flower helps attract in a balanced setting. Your awareness will be brought to your heart center so that you can recognize the love that always surrounds you. You don't need to look for it from someone else because you have been receiving it all along. Passionflower reminds you that you're never alone, and connects you to the compassion and support of the angels.

Message from Passionflower: "I open your crown chakra so you may connect to the unlimited supply of universal, unconditional, Divine love surrounding you. You needn't feel alone; the comfort and peace of Heaven is with you always. I open your heart so you'll feel the presence of the angels; remember to ask for their help whenever you need them. Call upon me if you feel stuck or you don't know which direction to take next. I'll attune you to the energy of the angels, who will give you guidance. I can bring these Divine beings very close to you so you'll hear their messages more clearly. Let's take your God-given gifts to greater heights."

Peony

Botanical Name: *Paeonia* spp.

Common Varieties: Common European peony (*Paeonia officinalis*) and Chinese peony (*Paeonia lactiflora*)

Energetic Properties: Distance healing, sending love, support for future times, healing conflict abroad, and enhancing energy

Associated Archangels: Raphael and Sandalphon

Associated Chakras: Root, sacral, and heart

Healing Description: Use Peony to arrange a support system for yourself when you know you will need it in the future. This is perfect for situations such as surgery, an interview, or an important meeting. Simply call on Peony, and ask that it grant you assistance during that time.

The energy of Peony is of love and healing, which makes it perfect for sending the benefits of Flower Therapy to others. You can use it on its own or combine it with other blossoms for distance healing. For example, if your friend is seeking a romantic relationship, you can create a bouquet of red roses and Peonies.

Message from Peony: "I hear your heart calling out to your family and friends living far away. I'll join you now in sending healing prayers and thoughts. Rest assured that your loved ones are receiving the blessings you're sending, because the energy travels through the network of the angels. No matter how great the distance, it will be like you're there with them. Imagine holding their hands and giving comforting hugs.

"I can help anyone move through their current situation. I'll even heal regions or countries experiencing troubled times and negative energy. The process is simple: sit with me, place your dominant hand near my petals, then ask for assistance for your loved ones or an area in need."

Peruvian Lily

Alternative Name: Lily of the Incas

Botanical Name: *Alstroemeria* spp.

Common Variety: New Zealand Christmas bell or parrot flower (*Alstroemeria psittacina*)

Energetic Properties: Clearing the energy of competition, allowing you to see the other side of the story, and releasing ego-based thoughts

Associated Archangels: Michael and Raguel

Associated Chakra: Root

Healing Description: The Peruvian Lily brings balance and calm into your life. It helps you see things from other points of view, and eases the feeling that you need to be in competition with others. These important steps will clear your ego's energy and help you move higher up the spiritual ladder. The Peruvian Lily reminds you to focus on the love that's all around you. You needn't fear loss, because the Universe will ensure that you and your family are always supported. Ask for the angels' assistance, and they will bring even greater abundance into your life.

Message from Peruvian Lily: "Express yourself through love and joy, not through the lower energy of competition.

Competition plays on the ego's view that there's not enough for everyone, and that we must take from others in order to be successful. Don't buy into this idea of 'lack,' for you are truly abundant in every aspect of life. God and the angels will provide you with all you could ever want or need if you remember to ask them.

"I also ask you to see things from other people's perspectives. Sometimes we can be so sure of ourselves that we miss the point or completely ignore what another person is trying to say. I will remind you of the importance of balance."

Petunia

Alternative Name: Sunweed

Botanical Name: *Petunia* spp.

Energetic Properties: Increasing fun, joy, playfulness, and laughter; connecting you to the fairies; resolving conflict; and easing communication

Associated Archangels: Ariel, Gabriel, and Raguel

Associated Chakras: Root and heart

Healing Description: Petunias bring joy and laughter to everyone; plant them around your home to ensure you're always having fun. They help defuse tension and encourage better communication. While all flowers are associated with the fairies, Petunias have a deeper connection than most. They are also strongly linked with Archangel Gabriel; the blossoms even look like little trumpets, which are the instruments Gabriel is associated with.

Message from Petunia: "The time for more play, laughter, and fun is *now!* Let me release the heavy energy of arguments and conflict that is standing in the way of your joy. I love bringing happiness to all those who are willing to receive it. Imagine how much more energy you'd have if you had more fun. That is why I'm here: to help usher in lighthearted energy so you can enjoy every moment of every day. I also improve communication and help you express yourself in positive ways."

Pig Face

Alternative Name: Ice plant

Botanical Name: *Carpobrotus glaucescens*

Energetic Properties: Increasing physical and emotional strength, resilience, building your business, and improving morale at work

Associated Archangels: Metatron and Michael

Associated Chakras: Root, sacral, and heart

Healing Description: Pig Face increases your physical and emotional strength. Working with this flower will help your body adjust to any exercise regimen and bring about lasting change. It grants you the emotional strength to walk with your head held high no matter what.

Pig Face also assists with your career. Your work life will become easier, and you'll receive promotions. Tasks in your workplace will be allocated smoothly, ensuring that you're able to do what you enjoy and leaving the stressful or tiring jobs for someone else who will appreciate them.

Message from Pig Face: "I bring you strength and resilience. I'll build you up when you feel fragile. You will not wither or falter; instead, you'll keep your chin up and continue on under all circumstances. You may not move quickly, but you *will* move forward.

"I'll also work with you, step-by-step, to progress in your career. I'll help you climb the corporate ladder if that is your desire. If you're self-employed, I'll bring you more clients. If you work for someone else, I can make your interpersonal relations easier. Let me take away the meaningless tasks from you and give them to someone who would enjoy them more so that you can achieve the things that make your heart truly happy."

Pine

Botanical Name: *Pinus* spp.

Energetic Properties: Emotional strength, self-confidence, removing negativity, more focused meditation, and protection

Associated Archangels: Michael and Raziel

Associated Chakras: Solar plexus, heart, and throat

Healing Description: The Pine is a majestic tree. Although pinecones are technically not a flower (they're the resulting seed), they make wonderful protective charms. Place them outside your door to keep out negativity. Then when people enter your home, they'll be accepting a spiritual contract to speak with love and treat you with respect. If you sit with Pine when you're feeling fragile, it will rebuild your strength and self-confidence.

Pine bonsai, like the one pictured here, make incredible meditation tools. They have all the qualities of Pine, and deepen your spiritual experience as well. When you're around them, you'll feel your strength grow.

Message from Pine: "I allow you to stand tall and hold your head high. I keep you emotionally stable. Never buy into the negativity of others. 'Words will never hurt me' will become your mantra. When people feel the need to verbally attack you, it reveals a lot more about their insecurities than about you. Don't give any further thought to how others view you, and become totally content with who you are. You're wonderful and kind.

"You'll soon notice a decrease in negative experiences as I protect you from lower vibrations and lower-resonating words. Everything that you hear and say is filtered through a veil of love, benefiting you and those around you."

Poinsettia

Botanical Name: *Euphorbia pulcherrima*

Energetic Properties: Finding and working toward your life purpose, inspiring others, and celebration

Associated Archangels: Haniel, Jophiel, and Raziel

Associated Chakra: Crown

Healing Description: The Poinsettia is a traditional Christmas flower, which isn't surprising when you feel its energy. It will guide you on the path of your life purpose and make you happier with each step you take. When you stray from your path, the energy of this healing friend reminds you of your mission. Use this flower at the end of the year to re-center yourself. The coming year will be filled with wonderful opportunities.

Message from Poinsettia: "You have an amazing purpose on this planet. The angels and I have been sending you feelings to guide you, so please follow your intuition and continue along the path of your life purpose. As you do so, a state of well-being will naturally come upon you, and this will create a beautiful ripple effect. When you live the life you wish, it inspires others and guides them onto their own Divine path.

"I'm also the flower of celebration! It's time to relax, have fun, and play."

Poppy

Botanical Name: *Papaver* spp.

Energetic Properties: Granting wishes, making dreams come true, and reminding you of the power of possibility

Associated Archangels: Raziel, Uriel, and Zadkiel

Associated Chakra: Crown

Healing Description: Poppies guide your desires to fruition, actively setting out to bring them into your physical reality. Your wishes become tangible. Try this method to manifest your desires with Poppies:

Gather some Poppy seeds from your local garden center or nursery. Go to where you want to plant them, either a flower bed or pot. Hold the seeds in your palm and visualize your wishes. Say: *"Poppies, please bring me these heartfelt desires as fast as you can. I'm ready to receive these gifts now. If you feel there's something even greater for me, I'm willing to accept this. Thank you."* Plant and gently water your seeds. As these Poppies begin to grow, your wishes will manifest.

Message from Poppy: "Wishes do come true! Your dreams are closer to being a reality than you think. You only have to ask, and you shall receive. I'll bring wonderful blessings to you right now. I remind you that you can have anything you desire; there's nothing outside your reach. Once you ask, simply allow me and your angels to create the perfect way for these blessings to be delivered. Open up your arms. Open your heart. You're about to receive!"

Portulaca

Alternative Names: Rose moss, purslane, and sun plant

Botanical Name: *Portulaca* spp.

Common Variety: *Portulaca grandiflora*

Energetic Properties: Improving your diet and releasing unhealthy foods

Associated Archangel: Raphael

Associated Chakra: Sacral

Healing Description: Portulaca doesn't hold back! You'd better be ready to make a commitment to change your lifestyle. This flower doesn't subtly hint that it's time to make a change; Portulaca demands it! Staying healthy helps you connect to your angelic friends.

Message from Portulaca: "It's now time for you to give up the junk food you've been indulging in. Each time you eat such items, it becomes harder to hear your angels. Imagine feeling good and full of energy; this is the life I see for you. Release the toxins from your diet and you'll be able to have the life you desire. I won't mess around; I'm all about getting the job done. Make a commitment to eliminate unhealthy foods from your diet; you know what they are! I'll ensure that you don't succumb to temptation. Instead, you'll take the road of joy."

Primula

Alternative Names: Polyanthus and primrose

Botanical Name: *Primula* spp.

Common Varieties: Common primrose (*Primula vulgaris*) and cowslip (*Primula veris*)

Energetic Properties: Healing for children, improving behavior, mastering schoolwork, and balancing energy

Associated Archangel: Metatron

Associated Chakras: All

Healing Description: Primula is not only easy to grow, it's easy to work with! This flower focuses its energy on guiding children. It's an excellent flower for Crystal or Indigo children because it helps sensitive ones become more balanced, focused, and grounded. It improves all children's behavior by aiding them in releasing negative energies they've absorbed.

Encourage your kids to grow and to take care of Primula. This simple, effective means of using Flower Therapy will help them balance their energy. You can also place pictures of Primula in their bedrooms if you can't have live plants.

Message from Primula: "Are you struggling to connect with your children? Do you feel they could be doing better at school? Let me help them while also helping you. You don't need to worry about them. I'll help to balance them in all ways. Children can be quiet and content one minute, then restless and irritated the next. This is because they are very sensitive, and easily pick up the energy of the people they're around and the environments they're in. We need to make this energy exchange more comfortable for them. Involve me in your children's Flower Therapy, and you'll find a quick, positive change in their personalities and schoolwork. Everyone will be cool, calm, and collected all day long."

Protea

Alternative Name: Sugarbush

Botanical Name: *Protea* spp.

Energetic Properties: Resolving grief energy, connecting with deceased loved ones, and feeling supported

Associated Archangel: Azrael

Associated Chakras: Root, sacral, and heart

Healing Description: Protea helps you move through the grief process. Whether the pain is old or new, this is an emotion that needs to be fully faced in order for you to get past it. Once you do, you will reignite your inner passions. Clear unresolved grief energy by surrounding yourself with Proteas. They will remind you that you're supported by your relatives and friends, and allow you to connect with those who have left this world. Feel the love that you are being sent from the Other Side.

Message from Protea: "I'm giving you the warm embrace you need right now. I'll help you slowly move through this and come out the other side a stronger person. Grief is a low form of energy, so try not to push it down further. Acknowledge your emotions, and allow your heart to heal fully. Feel yourself being surrounded by your loving support team of family, friends, and departed loved ones. They're very close to you right now, and they'll help you regain happiness. You've always been such an inspiration to others; reconnecting to your inner joy allows those around you to feel happier and lighter."

Rose *(Pink)*

Botanical Name: *Rosa* spp.

Energetic Properties: Beauty, self-confidence, comfort, and being content with yourself

Associated Archangel: Jophiel

Associated Chakras: Solar plexus and heart

Healing Description: Pink Roses increase your confidence and help you accept the beauty within yourself. You'll know everything is as it's meant to be, right now. Pink Roses guide you to fully accept yourself, which boosts your self-esteem. You needn't change anything about yourself at this time.

Message from Pink Rose: "You're perfect just the way you are. There's nothing you need to change in order to find true beauty. Let me help you love yourself: Look in a mirror and tell yourself that you're gorgeous, and *mean* it. Love everything about you. You're made in the image and likeness of God. There's nothing within your being that's imperfect, nothing within you that wasn't born from love."

Rose *(Red)*

Botanical Name: *Rosa* spp.

Energetic Properties: Attracting love, enhancing passion and romance, increasing motivation, and promoting healing

Associated Archangels: Haniel and Jophiel

Associated Chakras: Root, sacral, and heart

Healing Description: Archangel Jophiel, the angel of beauty, is frequently pictured with Roses in her hair. Red Roses are the epitome of love and passion, and a traditional romantic gift. There's always an abundance of these flowers around Valentine's Day. To open the heart chakra, sit with Red Roses. Whether you have a single long-stemmed Rose or a huge bouquet, the energy is essentially the same. Feel as this powerful healing energy effortlessly melts blockages in your heart. Now it will be easier to attract or enhance love in your life.

Message from Red Rose: "You deserve love; let me help you in this area. Together we will find the deep connection and passion you seek. You may have had some negative relationship experiences in this or a previous life. With your permission, I will heal those wounds and allow you to move forward with positivity. You will *become* the love you wish to experience."

Rose *(White)*

Botanical Name: *Rosa* spp.

Energetic Properties: Purification, peace, gentle transition, releasing links from the past, and clearing earthbound spirits

Associated Archangels: Metatron, Michael, and Raphael

Associated Chakra: Crown

Healing Description: White Roses are a symbol of purity and cleansing. This flower clears stagnant energy, so it's great to use in homes, offices, or sickrooms. You can call on its purifying capabilities to banish anything, from negative vibes to earthbound spirits. Simply place an odd number of Roses in a room, and Flower Therapy will cleanse the area. After losing a loved one, you can use White Roses to help you during this difficult transition to the next stage of life.

Message from White Rose: "I'll clear the energy of your aura. With your permission, I will help your energy shine as vividly as my own petals. I support you while gently releasing old, heavy energy attachments. I'll make you feel safe and protected, never fearful or hurt. Once you've been purified, you'll enjoy and appreciate a new state of peacefulness."

Rose (Yellow)

Botanical Name: *Rosa* spp.

Energetic Properties: Cultivating calm, peace, and joy; and concentration

Associated Archangels: Haniel and Uriel

Associated Chakras: Solar plexus, third eye, and crown

Healing Description: Yellow Roses allow you to find a place of peace within yourself, calming your mind so you can focus on the task at hand. This flower brings balance between work, rest, and play; it's perfect for students. Yellow Roses help you find fun and express your joy while still maintaining a sense of dignity and poise.

Message from Yellow Rose: "It's time for you to play! Find the joy in everything you do and everywhere you go. There's no need to concern yourself with thoughts of appearing too silly or childlike. I'll help you find happiness in ways that support your integrity. If you like, I can help you organize your thoughts and focus more clearly; this way, you have fun while still honoring your responsibilities."

Saint-John's-Wort

Botanical Name: *Hypericum perforatum*

Energetic Properties: Lifting depression, removing anxieties, releasing darkness, and lifting you above confusion

Associated Archangels: Metatron, Michael, and Raphael

Associated Chakras: Root, sacral, solar plexus, and heart

Healing Description: Saint-John's-Wort is renowned for its ability to ease anxiety and depression. It removes any cloudiness you may be feeling within your mind and lifts you to a place where you have enough energy and motivation to keep moving forward.

When the herb is taken medicinally, please be aware of potential interactions with pharmaceutical drugs. It shouldn't be used in conjunction with certain common antidepressants or birth-control pills. However, Flower Therapy has no direct interaction with medications of any kind, because you'll be working on an energetic level. Therefore, you can use this modality to safely invite the energy of Saint-John's-Wort into your life.

Message from Saint-John's-Wort: "I'm like a bright, shining light whose rays reach down to you at the bottom of a pit to dispel the darkness. I can see there's a lot of confusion, and you're surrounded by complicated events right now. I will lift you above this obscurity and show you the brightness you can achieve. Now is the time to release any hold that depression or anxiety has on you. However, please be gentle and try not to push yourself too much. I'll bring you the energy, state of mind, and motivation to move past your current darkness, into the light."

Scaevola

Alternative Names: Fan flower, half-flower, and naupaka

Botanical Name: *Scaevola* spp.

Energetic Properties: Connectedness, removing feelings of isolation, dispelling loneliness, and sending healing to loved ones

Associated Archangels: Azrael and Michael

Associated Chakras: Root and sacral

Healing Description: Scaevola clears away feelings of loneliness and helps you recognize that you are connected to every other person on the planet. Allow this thought to bring you comfort. Trust that you're being Divinely guided, protected, and assisted at every moment.

Use this flower when you're missing someone. This may be a loved one who lives far away or is traveling—or even deceased. Scaevola helps heal your emotions, and reminds you that the people you care about can feel your love no matter where they are.

Message from Scaevola: "Let me give you the comfort you need now. I sense you're feeling lonely and separated from your peers. Please remember that you are never alone; we are each connected at a deep soul level at every moment of every day. You're always supported by God and the angels in each thought you have and every decision you make. Allow me to reconnect you to the loving light of God. You'll once again feel part of the whole. Don't worry about your loved ones either; they, too, are protected by the Divine. The angels and I are sending them your love at this very moment."

Snapdragon

Botanical Name: *Antirrhinum* spp.

Energetic Properties: Communication; releasing anger, hate, and resentment; healing your voice; and enhancing the love in your words

Associated Archangels: Jophiel, Metatron, Michael, and Raphael

Associated Chakras: Heart and throat

Healing Description: Snapdragon helps you clear negativity and bring balance and love into your center. When you communicate, you'll no longer feel lower energies.

When you have a Snapdragon blossom on hand, you can use it to release lower emotions in this way: Write your concerns on a tiny piece of paper. A single word or a couple of short sentences will suffice. Fold the paper as many times as you can. Gently squeeze the sides of the flower until it opens up (you'll notice it looks similar to a dragon's mouth!), and place your paper inside. You'll instantly feel a release. Now take the Snapdragon to a quiet spot in the garden or a park, and ceremoniously toss the flower on the ground. With it, let the tension go!

Message from Snapdragon: "I'm here to heal your voice. I remind you to incorporate love into all of your communications. I understand that you've been thinking harsh things at times. I can dissolve this heavy energy. Let me bring your focus back to a place of love and balance. It's best not to say negative or hurtful words to others. As a human being, you'll occasionally have unkind thoughts, but it's important not to give power to the negativity by vocalizing them. Allow me to clear that energy from you and help you stay on the path of peace."

Sunflower

Botanical Name: *Helianthus annuus*

Energetic Properties: Raising moods, lifting energy levels, and promoting smiles and happiness

Associated Archangels: Jophiel and Michael

Associated Chakra: Solar plexus

Healing Description: Sunflowers exude joy. You can't help but smile when you see a cheerful, vibrant Sunflower. Notice how each blossom has a dark center and radiant yellow petals, representing the lightness that this flower can bring to you even when you feel at your lowest, or "darkest." When it feels like everything is a struggle, gather some healing Sunflowers. You'll feel your mood and energy levels shift right away.

Message from Sunflower: "I know there were times in the past when you felt exhausted and low. Now is the time for change. Let me banish this darkness; come into the light and see how beautiful the world can be. Remember how wonderful it feels to be happy, and enjoy each day to the fullest. Be happy with who you are. I'll support you in coming to terms with every aspect of yourself. You're shining as brightly as the sun, and it's time to cast that light on everyone and everything around you."

Sweet Pea

Botanical Name: *Lathyrus odoratus*

Energetic Properties: Manifestation, granting wishes, and trusting in prayer

Associated Archangels: Jophiel, Raziel, and Sandalphon

Associated Chakras: Root, sacral, and heart

Healing Description: This flower helps attract all your desires, and the things you need right *now* will come the fastest. You should always reach for the stars—the absolute best outcome that you can imagine.

Try this method for granting wishes: Sit with some Sweet Pea seeds, and really focus on your desire. Infuse the seeds with these loving intentions, then plant them in a garden bed or pot. As the seeds sprout and grow, reaching higher and higher, the energy they contain continues to build as well. When the blossoms finally emerge, their energy will be sent into the Universe, and your wish will be granted.

Message from Sweet Pea: "I can help you give birth to all of your exciting ideas and heartfelt desires. As I blossom, so too do your goals and aspirations. Accept these fulfilled wishes as a natural part of your life. You certainly deserve to receive them right now! You don't have to do anything else at this point; simply focus on your wishes and trust that they're being delivered to you. Believe that anything is possible and miracles are just an everyday occurrence. You can live the life you desire."

Tulip

Botanical Name: *Tulipa* spp.

Energetic Properties: Grace, poise, calm, removing irritations, releasing anger, and preventing interruptions

Associated Archangels: Haniel, Raguel, and Zadkiel

Associated Chakras: Root, sacral, solar plexus, and crown

Healing Description: Tulips clear out energies that cause annoyance and anger. These calming flowers help you relax and focus better, even when circumstances seem to be conspiring to prevent you from completing your work (such as when a loved one or co-worker is constantly interrupting with requests for aid). When you feel like you aren't making any progress, the energy of Tulips helps bring balance, and everything comes back into order.

Message from Tulip: "Allow your body to absorb my healing energies. Let go of any harsh emotions you're experiencing. Call on me when you don't have time for yourself or your work. There's no better time than now to benefit from my healing energies. I'll support you, and allow you to carry yourself with grace and poise."

Waratah

Botanical Name: *Telopea specio-sissima*

Energetic Properties: Protection, passion, spiritual understanding, trusting your guidance, finding your life purpose, overcoming obstacles, and courage

Associated Archangels: Michael, Raziel, and Sandalphon

Associated Chakras: Solar plexus and crown

Healing Description: Waratah is an Australian flower that's been admired for centuries. When it was first discovered, botanists were awestruck. They gave it a botanical name that roughly translates to "beauty that can be enjoyed from a distance," because the bright red Waratah can be seen even from very far away. Its blossom looks like a cocoon, shielding and protecting its center. This perfectly represents Waratah's energetic properties. It tells you it's time to accept the role you were born into, and gives you courage to step onto your life's path. Waratah takes away any fears connected to achieving your life purpose, brings a sense of peace and trust, and allows you to move forward with conviction.

Message from Waratah: "It's time to experience the world in a joyous and loving way. I'll assist you in coming out of your shell and reignite the passion within. Accept the mission you've been given this lifetime; I will help you overcome any obstacles as you strive to reach the top. I have helped people come to terms with their spirituality for centuries, and I'll guide you in finding your purpose and connecting to Divine guidance."

Wattle

Alternative Names: Acacia and thorntree

Botanical Name: *Acacia* spp.

Energetic Properties: Increasing laughter, reminding you to play, bringing joy to everyone around you, and making parties fun and uplifting

Associated Archangels: Jophiel and Metatron

Associated Chakras: Root, heart, and crown

Healing Description: Blossoms cover the Wattle tree completely, so it looks like it's draped in a single bright yellow blanket, although it is actually made up of individual flowers. These small flowers make you feel good, but when grouped together, they make you feel *great*.

Begin working with the fun, uplifting energy of Wattle flowers and you'll soon find your life filled with joy and laughter. Just as the tiny blossoms burst open with brightness, you, too, will bask in the glow of its healing energy . . . and help others through your own delight.

Message from Wattle: "I'll help you burst forth with joy! You'll find yourself laughing more and more when working with me. Each day brings only greater happiness. You're spreading laughter wherever you go, and others will soon comment on how fun you are to be around. I'll make the energy in your workplace lighter and more balanced. If you host any kind of social gathering, invoke my energy, and we will make it a wonderful time for everyone involved."

Wisteria

Alternative Name: Wistaria

Botanical Name: *Wisteria* spp.

Common Variety: Chinese wisteria (*Wisteria sinensis*)

Energetic Properties: Distance healing, protection, increasing focus and energy, raising your levels of spirituality, decision making, and clearing procrastination

Associated Archangels: Jeremiel and Michael

Associated Chakras: Third eye and crown

Healing Description: Use Wisteria for distance work, including healing. This plant helps you move higher along your spiritual evolution. It keeps your head clear by guiding you to abstain from artificial substances and other things that negatively impact your energy. Wisteria also helps with making decisions. If you are confused at all, you might then procrastinate, preventing you from making *any* decision. Wisteria, however, provides you with direction and helps you choose the perfect path each and every time.

Message from Wisteria: "I guide you each step of the way as you rise up the ladder of spirituality and personal development. I'll cast out all doubt and fear. Each decision you make will allow you to blossom into an even more beautiful version of yourself. Your energy is raised, and your vitality is pure. I help you connect with those who are separated from you; I'll deliver your wishes and positive thoughts across the barriers of time and space. Know that you're just as close to that person now as you've ever been."

PART III

FLOWER THERAPY CHARTS

ARCHANGEL
ASSOCIATIONS
WITH FLOWERS

Archangel Ariel

Agapanthus
Bluebell
Heather
Petunia

Archangel Azrael

Banksia
Pansy
Protea
Scaevola

Archangel Chamuel

African Violet
Banksia
Camellia
Chrysanthemum
Hibiscus
Hyacinth
Lantana
Magnolia, pink

Archangel Gabriel

Anthurium
Bird-of-Paradise

Crab Apple
Daffodil
Dianthus
Grevillea
Lantana
Petunia

Archangel Haniel

Carnation
Cherry Blossom
Lavender
Lily of the Valley
Magnolia, pink
Poinsettia
Rose, red
Rose, yellow
Tulip

Archangel Jeremiel

Black-eyed Susan
Camellia
Clover
Gerbera
Grevillea
Hydrangea
Lavender

Lily, pink
Moonflower
Orchid
Wisteria

Archangel Jophiel

Anthurium
Bleeding Heart
Calla Lily
Camellia
Carnation
Cherry Blossom
Dandelion
Dianthus
Gladiolus
Jonquil
Lily, orange
Mandevilla
Poinsettia
Rose, pink
Rose, red
Snapdragon
Sunflower
Sweet Pea
Wattle

Archangel Metatron

African Violet
Baby's Breath
Bird-of-Paradise
Bottlebrush
Cactus
Daisy
Dianthus
Eucalyptus
Frangipani
Fuchsia
Gardenia
Geranium
Jonquil
Lily, yellow
Lotus
Magnolia, white
Mandevilla
Marigold
Nasturtium
Pansy
Pig Face
Primula
Rose, white
Saint-John's-Wort
Snapdragon
Wattle

Archangel Michael

African Violet
Baby's Breath
Bottlebrush
Bougainvillea
Bromeliad
Cactus
Daffodil
Dahlia
Delphinium
Dianthus
Echinacea
Eucalyptus
Freesia
Fuchsia
Gardenia
Geranium
Gladiolus
Iris
Jonquil
Lavender
Lilac
Lily, yellow
Magnolia, white
Mandevilla
Marigold
Pansy

Peruvian Lily
Pig Face
Pine
Rose, white
Scaevola
Saint-John's-Wort
Snapdragon
Sunflower
Waratah
Wisteria

Archangel Raguel

Banksia
Chrysanthemum
Dandelion
Gerbera
Lantana
Peruvian Lily
Petunia
Tulip

Archangel Raphael

African Violet
Agapanthus
Banksia
Begonia

Black-eyed Susan
Bleeding Heart
Bottlebrush
Cactus
Calendula
Camellia
Daffodil
Dandelion
Dianthus
Eucalyptus
Freesia
Gardenia
Geranium
Gladiolus
Hyacinth
Iris
Lily, yellow
Magnolia, white
Pansy
Peony
Portulaca
Rose, white
Saint-John's-Wort
Snapdragon

Archangel Raziel

Azalea
Black-eyed Susan
Cactus
Clover
Crocus
Dandelion
Eucalyptus
Forget-me-not
Frangipani
Hibiscus
Jasmine
Lavender
Lily, pink
Lotus
Passionflower
Pine
Poinsettia
Poppy
Sweet Pea
Waratah

Archangel Sandalphon

Black-eyed Susan
Bromeliad

Delphinium
Gardenia
Hydrangea
Moonflower
Nasturtium
Orchid
Peony
Sweet Pea
Waratah

Archangel Uriel

Baby's Breath
Clover
Dianthus
Iris
Poppy
Rose, yellow

Archangel Zadkiel

Dahlia
Poppy
Tulip

CHAKRA
ASSOCIATIONS
WITH FLOWERS

All Chakras

Baby's Breath
Dianthus
Lotus
Primula

Root

Agapanthus
Baby's Breath
Banksia
Begonia
Bougainvillea

Carnation
Chrysanthemum
Clover
Crab Apple
Dahlia
Daisy
Dandelion
Delphinium
Dianthus
Eucalyptus
Freesia
Fuchsia
Gardenia

Grevillea
Heather
Hibiscus
Hyacinth
Hydrangea
Lavender
Lily, yellow
Lotus
Magnolia, pink
Mandevilla
Peony
Peruvian Lily
Petunia
Pig Face
Primula
Protea
Rose, red
Saint-John's-Wort
Scaevola
Sweet Pea
Tulip
Wattle

Sacral

Baby's Breath
Banksia
Begonia
Bluebell

Bottlebrush
Camellia
Crab Apple
Daisy
Delphinium
Dianthus
Fuchsia
Gerbera
Heather
Hyacinth
Hydrangea
Iris
Lily, pink
Lily, yellow
Lotus
Magnolia, pink
Magnolia, white
Nasturtium
Orchid
Peony
Pig Face
Portulaca
Primula
Protea
Rose, red
Saint-John's-Wort
Scaevola
Sweet Pea
Tulip

Solar Plexus

Baby's Breath
Banksia
Begonia
Black-eyed Susan
Bluebell
Bottlebrush
Cactus
Calendula
Camellia
Chrysanthemum
Daisy
Delphinium
Dianthus
Freesia
Fuchsia
Gerbera
Gladiolus
Hydrangea
Lavender
Lilac
Lily, orange
Lily, pink
Lily, yellow
Lotus
Marigold
Nasturtium
Pine
Primula

Rose, pink
Rose, yellow
Saint-John's-Wort
Sunflower
Tulip
Waratah

Heart

Anthurium
Baby's Breath
Banksia
Black-eyed Susan
Bleeding Heart
Bottlebrush
Cactus
Calendula
Calla lily
Camellia
Carnation
Cherry Blossom
Chrysanthemum
Clover
Daffodil
Dandelion
Dianthus
Fuchsia
Gardenia
Gerbera
Gladiolus

Heather
Hibiscus
Iris
Lantana
Lotus
Magnolia, pink
Orchid
Passionflower
Peony
Petunia
Pig Face
Pine
Primula
Protea
Rose, pink
Rose, red
Saint-John's-Wort
Snapdragon
Sweet Pea
Wattle

Throat

Anthurium
Baby's Breath
Bird-of-Paradise
Daffodil
Dandelion
Dianthus

Eucalyptus
Grevillea
Lantana
Lotus
Marigold
Pine
Primula
Snapdragon

Third Eye

African Violet
Baby's Breath
Bird-of-Paradise
Bromeliad
Cactus
Crocus
Daffodil
Delphinium
Dianthus
Echinacea
Eucalyptus
Forget-me-not
Frangipani
Geranium
Grevillea
Jasmine
Jonquil
Lavender

Lotus
Pansy
Passionflower
Primula
Rose, yellow
Wisteria

Crown

African Violet
Azalea
Baby's Breath
Bird-of-Paradise
Bottlebrush
Bromeliad
Cactus
Camellia
Clover
Crocus
Dahlia
Daisy
Dandelion
Delphinium
Dianthus
Eucalyptus

Forget-me-not
Frangipani
Gardenia
Geranium
Hibiscus
Iris
Jasmine
Jonquil
Lily of the Valley
Lotus
Magnolia, pink
Marigold
Moonflower
Orchid
Passionflower
Poinsettia
Poppy
Primula
Rose, white
Rose, yellow
Tulip
Waratah
Wattle
Wisteria

ENERGETIC HEALING PROPERTIES OF FLOWERS

Addictions, Releasing

Agapanthus
Iris
Magnolia, white

All-Purpose Flower

Baby's Breath
Dianthus

Angels, Connecting with

Bird-of-Paradise
Frangipani
Gardenia
Lotus
Passionflower

Anger, Releasing

Begonia
Dandelion
Snapdragon
Tulip

Animals, Healing

Heather

Anxiety, Removing

Lavender
Lilac
Saint-John's-Wort

Aura Strengthening

Calendula
Geranium
Jonquil
Nasturtium

Beauty, Enhancing

Rose, pink

Behavior, Improving

Primula

Business, Increasing Your

Pig Face

Calmness, Bringing

Begonia
Daisy
Freesia
Fuchsia
Gardenia
Hibiscus
Jasmine
Jonquil
Lavender
Lilac
Lily, orange
Rose, yellow
Tulip

Celebration

Poinsettia
Wattle

Chakra Clearing

Bird-of-Paradise
Lotus

Children, Healing

Daffodil
Primula

Clairvoyance, Enhancing

Echinacea
Lavender
Pansy

Commitment

Carnation
Lily, pink

Communication, Enhancing

Bird-of-Paradise
Daffodil
Petunia
Snapdragon

Competition, Clearing the Energy of

Peruvian Lily

Completing Assignments

Daffodil
Primula
Rose, yellow

Cycles, Breaking

Moonflower

Courage

Waratah

Deceased Loved Ones, Connecting to

Bird-of-Paradise
Protea

Depression

Black-eyed Susan
Gardenia
Gladiolus
Lilac
Lily, orange
Saint-John's-Wort
Sunflower

Desires, Achieving Your

Delphinium
Dianthus
Eucalyptus
Grevillea
Orchid

Poppy
Sweet Pea

Diet, Moving to a Healthier

Portulaca

Earthbound Spirits, Clearing

Rose, white

Electromagnetic Radiation, Clearing

Magnolia, white

Energy, Increasing Your

Frangipani
Geranium
Gladiolus
Iris
Petunia

Environmental Healing

Agapanthus
Bluebell
Magnolia, white

Fairies, Connecting with the

Bluebell
Petunia

Families, Healing

Chrysanthemum
Hibiscus
Lantana

Fertility

Grevillea
Magnolia, pink

Fidelity

Carnation

Financial Abundance

Clover
Lily, yellow
Nasturtium

Focus

Hyacinth
Rose, yellow
Wisteria

Forgiveness

Bleeding Heart

Friendships

Gerbera

Global Healing

Agapanthus
Peony

God, Connecting with

Bromeliad
Frangipani
Lotus
Passionflower

Grace

Cherry Blossom
Lily of the Valley
Tulip

Grief, Healing

Calla Lily
Camellia
Gladiolus

Pansy
Protea

Happiness

Bluebell
Calendula
Daisy
Dianthus
Gardenia
Gladiolus
Hibiscus
Jonquil
Petunia
Rose, yellow
Sunflower
Wattle

Harmony

Agapanthus
Chrysanthemum
Hibiscus
Lantana

Healing

Cactus
Calendula

Freesia (especially the
   back and spine)
Peony (especially from
   a distance)
Rose, red
Scaevola
Wisteria (from a
   distance)

Heart, Healing the

Bleeding Heart
Gladiolus

Help, Asking for

Clover
Eucalyptus
Poppy

Honesty

Lily of the Valley

House, Clearing the Energy of

African Violet
Jonquil

Ideas, Developing

Crab Apple
Sweet Pea

Intentions, Discovering Others'

Cherry Blossom

Jealousy, Releasing

Dandelion

Joy (see Happiness)

Life Purpose

Dahlia
Hyacinth
Poinsettia
Waratah

Love

Anthurium
Calla Lily
Camellia
Carnation

Cherry Blossom
Dianthus
Passionflower
Peony
Rose, red

Loyalty (see *Fidelity*)

Magnifying Energy

Baby's Breath
Peony

Making a Difference

Dahlia

Manifestation

Dianthus
Eucalyptus
Jasmine
Sweet Pea

Meditation, Enhancing

Azalea
Jasmine
Pine

Men's Health

Grevillea

Miracles

Eucalyptus
Sweet Pea

Money (see *Financial Abundance*)

Motivation

Bottlebrush
Fuchsia
Orchid
Rose, red
Saint-John's-Wort

Negativity, Clearing

African Violet
Black-eyed Susan
Bromeliad
Iris
Jonquil
Pine
Rose, white
Snapdragon

New Beginnings

Banksia

New Clients, Attracting

Pig Face

Obstacles, Overcoming

Marigold
Waratah

Old Emotions, Releasing

Black-eyed Susan
Bleeding Heart
Dandelion
Gladiolus
Hydrangea
Iris
Nasturtium
Saint-John's-Wort

Overwhelmed, Lifting Feelings of Being

Marigold

Passion, Enhancing

Anthurium
Rose, red
Waratah

Past-Life Healing

Azalea
Forget-me-not

Patience

Begonia

Perseverance

Clover
Fuchsia
Orchid

Personal Space

Mandevilla

Planets and Stars, Connecting to

Forget-me-not
Passionflower

Playfulness

Bluebell
Dianthus
Gardenia
Petunia
Wattle

Positive Thoughts

Bromeliad
Jonquil
Peruvian Lily

Procrastination, Removing

Hyacinth
Hydrangea
Marigold
Wisteria

Promotions, Attracting

Pig Face

Protection

Bougainvillea
Cactus

Delphinium (while in
   the ocean)
Geranium
Jonquil
Nasturtium
Pine
Waratah
Wisteria

Psychic Readings, Help with Giving

Bird-of-Paradise
Echinacea
Frangipani

Purification

African Violet
Rose, white

Relationships, Healing

Black-eyed Susan
Cherry blossom

Resentment, Releasing

Dandelion
Snapdragon

Romance

Anthurium
Calla Lily
Camellia
Cherry Blossom
Dianthus
Passionflower
Rose, red

Self-Confidence, Boosting

Rose, pink

Self-Esteem, Increasing

Black-eyed Susan
Calendula
Lily, orange
Mandevilla
Pine

Sibling Rivalry, Clearing

Chrysanthemum
Lantana

Simplifying Life

Daisy

Sleep

Lavender

Soul-Mate Relationships

Calla Lily
Camellia
Carnation

Speeches, Help with Giving

Bird-of-Paradise
Crocus
Daffodil
Grevillea
Snapdragon

Spiritual Teacher, Enhancing Your Abilities as a

Crocus
Daffodil

Spirituality

Azalea
Cactus
Crocus
Echinacea
Frangipani
Jasmine
Lotus
Waratah
Wisteria

Strength

Cactus
Freesia
Orchid
Pig Face
Pine

Stress, Removing

Daisy
Freesia
Fuchsia
Gardenia
Jonquil
Lavender
Lilac
Lily of the Valley
Passionflower

Third-Eye Chakra, Clearing

Echinacea
Lavender
Pansy

Time, Freeing Up

Cactus
Daisy
Tulip

Toxins, Releasing

Black-eyed Susan
Bottlebrush
Dandelion
Iris
Magnolia, white

Transitions

Delphinium
Hydrangea
Jonquil
Rose, white

Trust

Crab Apple
Dahlia
Delphinium
Sweet Pea
Waratah

Unity

Hibiscus
Scaevola

Weight Loss

Lily, orange

Wisdom

Azalea
Frangipani
Jasmine
Lotus

Wishes

Dandelion
Dianthus
Poppy
Sweet pea

Writing, Encouragement with

Daffodil
Grevillea

Words, Choosing More Loving

Anthurium
Bromeliad
Daffodil
Pine
Snapdragon

ACKNOWLEDGMENTS

From Doreen

Thank you to God for creating and giving us flowers, which are beautiful healing angels upon Earth. Flowers truly are God's masterpieces, and we are so blessed to have them in our lives.

I am deeply grateful to my co-author, Robert Reeves, for his dedication to Mother Nature, the flower kingdom, and the angelic realm (including the nature angels and elementals). Thank you, Robert, for your wonderful writing, editing, and support during the process of creating this book. Your wisdom as a naturopath, combined with your love and appreciation for nature, made this book possible. Thank you, also, to Andrew McGregor for your support during the writing and filming process.

A huge bouquet of gratitude to everyone at Hay House for bringing *Flower Therapy* to life. And lots of love to you for reading this book. May you receive bountiful blessings from every flower with whom you come into contact.

Love,
Doreen

From Robert

What an amazing dream come true this journey has been. I'm so happy and eternally grateful to be co-author of *Flower Therapy* with Doreen.

Thank you to my family. You've supported me throughout my journey. You've allowed me to grow and develop as I chose. It's because you let me be myself that I'm able to do this work. Without your constant love and support, my journey wouldn't have been possible. You're my rock, my love, and my constant. I know that I can always rely on each of you. Thank you.

Andrew, you've accepted me to the fullest extent. You've never tried to change me. This is just one of the reasons I love you.

I have been blessed with so many wonderful teachers. Each of them has taught me important lessons. I thank you for not looking at me as someone who is "too young." Instead, you supported me during my growth.

Thank you to Stirling Macoby for your book, *What Flower Is That?* (Lansdowne Press, 1986), which was invaluable in my research.

To my patients and clients who allowed me to follow my inner guidance, you let me trust in the angel messages I received. Together we allowed amazing healings to take place. I thank you for your support. Having the pleasure of supporting you on your healing journey is what truly makes me happy.

To Hay House, Louise L. Hay, Reid Tracy, Leon Nacson, Alex Freemon, and Nicolette Salamanca, thank you for allowing our joint vision to become a reality.

Doreen, where do I start? You're an amazing person. I am so grateful for your faith and trust in my becoming your co-author. This means so much more to me than words can express. I have loved every part of writing this book with you. I thank you for introducing me to the angelic realm. They've become wonderful friends that I rely on daily. I had the pleasure of meeting you in person in 2007, and the rest is history. I feel so lucky to call you one of my friends. With heartfelt gratitude, I thank you.

Of course I have to thank the angels and God for helping me with this project. Also, to nature for giving us the wonderful flowers that we can use for healing.

Many blessings,
Robert

ABOUT THE AUTHORS

Doreen Virtue is the best-selling author of *Fairies 101* and the *Magical Messages from Your Fairies Oracle Cards*. She's written numerous books about angels and has appeared on talk shows and other media internationally, including *Oprah, The View, Good Morning America,* CNN, the BBC, and *Kerri-Anne.* She lectures worldwide and is the host of a weekly call-in radio show on **HayHouseRadio.com**®.

Doreen holds three university degrees in counseling psychology and is a lifelong clairvoyant. She loves gardening and hiking outdoors in nature, especially among the wildflowers of Hawaii, where she lives.

Website: **www.AngelTherapy.com**

ANGEL THERAPY®

. . . .

Robert Reeves is a fully qualified and accredited naturopath with a special interest in mental and emotional health. He blends his herbal medicine and nutrition training with his psychic and mediumship abilities. He has a

strong connection to the angels and to the natural world, believing that nature holds the ability to heal when one is guided from the Divine.

Robert gives self-help workshops, writes magazine articles, and has been featured on international radio programs. He owns and runs a successful natural-therapies clinic in Australia, which he began when he was 17 years old. He has also developed a range of vibrational essences that focus on crystal and angel energy, and which are currently available as aura sprays.

Website: **www.robertreeves.com.au**

NOTES

NOTES

NOTES

NOTES

_____

_____

_____

_____

_____

_____

_____

_____

_____

_____

_____

_____

_____

_____

_____

_____

_____

_____

_____

NOTES

NOTES

Hay House Titles of Related Interest

YOU CAN HEAL YOUR LIFE, the movie,
starring Louise L. Hay & Friends
(available as a 1-DVD program and
an expanded 2-DVD set)
Watch the trailer at: **www.LouiseHayMovie.com**

THE SHIFT, the movie,
starring Dr. Wayne W. Dyer
(available as a 1-DVD program and
an expanded 2-DVD set)
Watch the trailer at: **www.DyerMovie.com**

AROMATHERAPY 101, by Karen Downes

***EARTH WISDOM: A Heart-Warming Mixture of the Spiritual
and the Practical,*** by Glennie Kindred

***GRACE, GUIDANCE, AND GIFTS: Sacred Blessings
to Light Your Way,*** by Sonia Choquette

***GREEN MADE EASY: The Everyday Guide for Transitioning
to a Green Lifestyle,*** by Chris Prelitz

***THE NATURE OF INFINITE LOVE & GRATITUDE
Transformation Cards,*** by Dr. Darren R. Weissman (card deck)

NATURE'S SECRET MESSAGES: Hidden in Plain Sight,
by Elaine Wilkes

All of the above are available at your local bookstore, or may be
ordered by contacting Hay House (see next page).

We hope you enjoyed this Hay House book.
If you'd like to receive our online catalog featuring
additional information on Hay House books and
products, or if you'd like to find out more
about the Hay Foundation, please contact:

Hay House, Inc., P.O. Box 5100, Carlsbad, CA 92018-5100
(760) 431-7695 or (800) 654-5126
(760) 431-6948 (fax) or (800) 650-5115 (fax)
www.hayhouse.com® • **www.hayfoundation.org**

Published and distributed in Australia by:
Hay House Australia Pty. Ltd., 18/36 Ralph St.,
Alexandria NSW 2015 • *Phone:* 612-9669-4299
Fax: 612-9669-4144 • www.hayhouse.com.au

Published and distributed in the United Kingdom by:
Hay House UK, Ltd., 292B Kensal Rd., London W10 5BE • *Phone:*
44-20-8962-1230 • *Fax:* 44-20-8962-1239 • www.hayhouse.co.uk

Published and distributed in the Republic of South Africa by:
Hay House SA (Pty), Ltd., P.O. Box 990, Witkoppen 2068
Phone/Fax: 27-11-467-8904 • www.hayhouse.co.za

Published in India by: Hay House Publishers India, Muskaan
Complex, Plot No. 3, B-2, Vasant Kunj, New Delhi 110 070
Phone: 91-11-4176-1620 • *Fax:* 91-11-4176-1630 • www.hayhouse.co.in

Distributed in Canada by: Raincoast, 9050 Shaughnessy St.,
Vancouver, B.C. V6P 6E5 • *Phone:* (604) 323-7100
Fax: (604) 323-2600 • www.raincoast.com

Take Your Soul on a Vacation

Visit **www.HealYourLife.com®** to regroup,
recharge, and reconnect with your own magnificence.
Featuring blogs, mind-body-spirit news, and
life-changing wisdom from Louise Hay and friends.

Visit **www.HealYourLife.com** today!